PHILOSOPHY IN LATE ANTIQUITY

Some of the most significant cultural achievements of Late Antiquity lie in the domains of philosophy and religion. Outstanding among these achievements was the establishment and development of Neoplatonism as one of the chief vehicles of thought, acting as a channel for the transmission of ancient philosophy to the medieval and renaissance worlds. Important, too, was the emergence of a distinctive Christian philosophy and theology based on a foundation of Greek pagan thinking.

Philosophy in Late Antiquity provides an essential new introduction to the key ideas of the Neoplatonists which affected approaches to Plato as late as the nineteenth century. Andrew Smith also shows how they influenced Christian thought. His approach not only allows us to appreciate these philosophical ideas in their own right, it also gives us significant insights into the mentality of the age which produced them.

Andrew Smith has been Professor of Classics in University College Dublin since 1992. His main interest is Greek philosophy, especially Neoplatonism; his previous publications include *Porphyry's Place in the Neoplatonic Tradition* (1974) and the Teubner edition of Porphyry's fragments (1993).

PHILOSOPHY IN LATE ANTIQUITY

Andrew Smith

Routledge
Taylor & Francis Group
LONDON AND NEW YORK

First published 2004
by Routledge
2 Park Square, Milton Park, Abingdon, Oxfordshire, OX14 4RN
Simultaneously published in the USA and Canada
by Routledge
29 West 35th Street, New York, NY 10001

Routledge is an imprint of the Taylor & Francis Group

Typeset in Garamond by
Rosemount Typing Services, Barjarg Tower, Auldgirth, Dumfriesshire
Printed and bound in Great Britain by
TJ International Ltd, Padstow, Cornwall

British Library Cataloguing in Publication Data
A catalogue record for this book is available from the British Library

Library of Congress Cataloging in Publication Data
Smith, Andrew, 1945–
Philosophy in late antiquity / Andrew Smith.
p. cm.
Includes bibliographical references and index.
1. Neoplatonism. 2. Philosophy and religion–History–To 1500.
3. Christianity–Philosophy–History–To 1500. I.
Title

B517.S65 2004
186'.4–dc22

2004000761

ISBN 0–415–225108 (hbk)
ISBN 0–415–225116 (pbk)

TO FREYA AND KATIE

CONTENTS

PREFACE

The intention in writing this book is to provide a general introduction to and encounter with the philosophy of Late Antiquity which will stimulate the reader to further study both in secondary sources and particularly in the reading of the original texts. The first task was to define what is meant by Late Antiquity in chronological terms and then to decide on which philosophers to include within that range. The two are not unconnected. I have decided to dwell almost exclusively on the thought of the Neoplatonist philosophers for three reasons. Of all the philosophers active in this period their thought was the most innovative. They also absorbed the thought of many other schools of philosophy, particularly that of the Stoics and Aristotelians. Indeed despite the continuing hostility of Platonists to some Aristotelian doctrines there was a developing concept of the consensus and harmony of Platonic and Aristotelian ideas. In fact the logical works of Aristotle became the standard introductory material for students in the Neoplatonic schools which gave rise to the publication of numerous commentaries on works of Aristotle. And last, both because they absorbed all other ancient thought and because they happened to flourish in the final phase of the pagan Greco-Roman world, they had an enormous influence on the subsequent development of philosophy. It is, of course, not to be denied that Aristotelians and to some extent Stoics continued to philosophise and that many people led their lives in accordance with their prescriptions. And here one should not ignore the Epicureans. But the main philosophical characteristics of their thinking had been largely established by the middle of the second century AD.

If Neoplatonism, then, is the dominant intellectual movement of Late Antiquity it seemed obvious to begin with its founder Plotinus in the third century AD: a century which may also be seen as a transition period because of the rapidity of economic and social change during its course. It is true that Plotinus' thought comes at the end of a long period of development in Platonic thought through the period we now call Middle-Platonism. But this is another story, beyond the scope of this book, which we can do no more than mention. Because of the overriding stature of Plotinus as a critical and creative thinker I have dedicated much of this book to him. This constitutes Part I which is intended to provide a fairly comprehensive introduction to the main philosophical concerns of Late Antique philosophy. Part II then takes up the story after Plotinus with an introductory chapter on philosophy and religion. Plotinus was in some ways exceptional in his apparent lack of interest in formal religion (he was of course an intense mystic), but the reconciliation and ultimate integration of pagan religious practice and philosophy was one of the most serious concerns of later Neoplatonists. A further chapter deals with the more purely philosophical developments of ideas which find their starting point or their particular formulation in Plotinus' work. Finally I have followed some of these central ideas in the work of a representative number of Christian thinkers whom I have treated more for their importance as philosophers than as theologians. Our period is closed by Boethius and Dionysius the Areopagite: not only for chronological reasons, but because they transmitted many of the leading philosophical ideas of Late Antiquity to a new age, through the Latin-speaking West and the Greek-speaking East respectively.

This introduction is not intended to be an exhaustive handbook or compendium of the history of thought, or even of Neoplatonism, in Late Antiquity. Rather, I have attempted to follow the development of a limited number of important and characteristic ideas. Although this will inevitably be selective, it seemed preferable to an attempt to cover every philosophical concept: an enterprise that would have quickly degenerated into a desiccated summary-list of concepts. I have also frequently cited the ancient authors because translations of some of them are hard to come by and, even when available, often difficult to find one's way around. I hope that the inclusion of the philosophers' own words will not only enliven the text but also stimulate readers to search further for themselves in the originals. They will also help to bring to our attention the vitality of these thinkers and something of their commitment to their own ideas, for above all they wanted to engage with their audiences and change their lives for the better.

I would finally like to thank John Dillon and Joan Wright for reading sections of the manuscript and giving me their advice.

Part I

SETTING THE AGENDA

The philosophy of Plotinus

INTRODUCTION

After Plato and Aristotle, Plotinus is arguably the greatest philosopher of antiquity and certainly one of the most influential. His particular interpretation of Plato set the guidelines for the next three hundred years and those Platonists who followed (Porphyry, Iamblichus, Proclus) kept close to the general outlines of his thought. He is therefore rightly regarded as the major instigator of a movement in Platonic philosophy whose innovative nature has since the nineteenth century been recognised with the title of Neoplatonism. Yet, perhaps even more influential was his indirect influence, which ensured that Plato was, until the early nineteenth century, largely read in the spirit of Plotinus. Plotinus' thought, however, did not spring fully armed from the head of Zeus, but was the culmination of a long period of development in Platonic and Pythagorean circles. By the second century BC Plato's Academy was firmly in the hands of a group of Platonists who gave more emphasis to the aporetic side of Plato's work and thus to the early dialogues in which Socrates played a more prominent role. A figure such as Carneades astonished his Roman audience by arguing for opposite views of Justice on two consecutive days. Their ethics was characterised by 'reasonableness', and their epistemology by the notion of suspension of judgement. By the first century BC, however, there had begun a return to the more positive doctrines of Platonic metaphysics. Philo of Larissa and Antiochus of Ascalon pointed the way. Antiochus was also heavily influenced by Stoicism and this combination of philosophical ideas was to become more and more characteristic of philosophical activity in the first centuries of the Roman Empire. Pythagoreanism also saw a revival. And when we consider that Plato himself was thought to have been influenced greatly by Pythagorean ideas, it is not difficult to see that Platonism and the revived Pythagoreanism could be mutually influential. One of the most important figures was Eudorus who seems to have developed the notion of a unitary first principle. A later advocate of Pythagoreanism, Numenius, also owed much to Plato and might as easily be considered a Platonist. His works were avidly studied by some of Plotinus' circle. At the same time the study of Aristotle was not neglected. A distinguished line of Peripatetics continued to comment on the works of Aristotle. Some, such as Alexander of Aphrodisias, even developed Aristotle's ideas.

Plotinus was himself extraordinarily well-read both in the philosophy of the early period and in more recent work. He knew the writings of Aristotle as intimately as the Platonic texts themselves[1] and we know that the commentaries and works of near contemporaries would be read aloud as the starting point for discussions in his own philosophical seminar.[2] Born, probably in Lycopolis, in Egypt in AD 205 he was naturally attracted to the cosmopolitan city of Alexandria, although he did not commence a formal education in philosophy until he was twenty-eight years old. No doubt he took the opportunities offered in Alexandria to acquaint himself with the teachings of Platonists, Aristotelians, Stoics and Epicureans. He had a deep attachment to his otherwise unknown teacher Ammonius Saccas who was perhaps partly responsible for Plotinus' more critical and original approach to philosophy. After about nine years' study in Alexandria he signed up with the emperor Gordian III's eastern expedition, ostensibly to make contact with the Brahmans, but seems to have extricated himself from the ensuing catastrophe (Gordian was killed in Mesopotamia), for he was able to make his way via Antioch to Rome, where probably under the patronage of the new emperor and philhellene Gallienus, he set up a philosophical school in the Roman residence of an aristocratic lady, Gemina. It is important from the outset to realise that the school was hardly a quiet haven. Plotinus' students included many professional men, politicians and doctors; he also acted as guardian for orphans of rich families whose primary education he personally supervised and whose accounts he kept in order. It is clear from Porphyry's *Life of Plotinus* that he provided for the moral and spiritual as well as the intellectual well-being of his companions. In fact these two sides are deeply interlaced in is thought.

The school or seminar of Plotinus was in no sense an official body like the Platonic Academy in Athens, whose directors would have seen themselves as the formal successors of Plato. There is no indication, for example, that the school continued after the death of

Plotinus in 270 AD. He would have regarded himself as a faithful Platonist expounding and clarifying the sometimes hidden implications of Plato's own words. But, although he was not without an awareness of some striking innovations, he probably genuinely thought that his often complete rethinking of Platonic metaphysics was an authentic representation of Plato's real meaning.

In one of his earliest treatises he makes clear his own position in the development of philosophy.[3] After referring to the Presocratics as precursors of his own thought he locates Plato as the central point of reference before moving on to Aristotle. The immediate context is a universal metaphysical framework which Plotinus sees implied dimly in the earliest philosophers and receiving its definitive expression, though not its fullest explication, in Plato. It is this work of clarifying Plato's ideas that Plotinus regarded as his philosophical task. And so he refined Plato's concepts of the Idea of the Good, the Forms and the Soul into his own succession of principles, the One, Intellect and Soul which he regarded as distinct entities or Hypostases (real beings). While Plato had strongly emphasised a two-world view consisting of the physical world and its ideal archetype represented by the Forms, he had not clearly and systematically divided the transcendent world into three levels.

But Plotinus' philosophising, like that of Plato, does not begin with these macrocosmic principles, but rather with the search for the nature of man himself, his soul and his destiny. In fact this very treatise both begins and ends with the individual. Thus from the beginning the question of our present state is posed:

> What is it, then, that has made the souls forget their father, God, and be ignorant of themselves and him, even though they are parts which come from his higher world and altogether belong to it?[4]

And at the end he encourages us to turn our attention inwards and upwards. This exhortation to a personal discovery of universal reality through the discovery of the self is a device frequently used to structure his philosophical enquiries. The philosophical point is that the self is in the end to be identified with the universal structure itself, i.e. with the Hypostases. But there is the further point that philosophical reflection begins with what is given in this world: the need for such a thing as intellect is argued from its being necessary for the existence of soul; and the need for the One from the necessity of unity to explain a world that is obviously unified and coherent.

More particularly, when Plotinus concerns himself with identifying our real self, what we are, he invariably begins with an attempt to identify the conscious human subject of feelings and thoughts in this physical world. A clear example is the very beginning of the late treatise which Porphyry places first in the collection:

> Pleasures and sadnesses, fears and assurances, desires and aversions and pain – whose are they? ... We must also consider intellectual acts and see how they take place and who or what they belong to, and observe what sort of thing it is that acts as overseer and carries out the investigation and comes to a decision about these matters. And first of all, who or what does sensation belong to? That is where we ought to begin, as feelings are either a sort of sensation or do not occur without sensation.[5]

For this reason, then, it is appropriate that we begin our exploration of the thought of Plotinus with his treatment of the individual soul. Only then will we move on to examine the universal context. The distinction is not always absolute since, after all, the individual intellect is under certain circumstances to be identified with the divine Intellect and frequently when he is discussing universal Soul or Intellect what he says may equally apply to the individual. After discussing the One and universal Intellect and Soul we will return once more to the individual, which is in keeping with the importance Plotinus places on the spiritual journey of the soul in its descent into the world and return to its origins.

1

THE INDIVIDUAL

Soul and body

Like the universe as a whole, man too consists of a material part, his body, and an immaterial element which Plotinus, following Plato, calls the 'inner man'.[1] In its most general application this 'inner man' encompasses the human soul and intellect as well as something of the ultimate principle, the One itself. The individual soul, too, can be further subdivided into a number of levels that correspond to the various activities which we commonly identify in the human being. At the lowest level there is the basic activity of life seen in the growth of the human body, something that man shares with plants. At a higher level is local movement, which is shared with animals. Above this come feelings, perceptions, memory and the exercise of discursive reason. In all of these activities the soul interacts with the body, not by being inside the body in a spatial sense, but by being present through its power which may be said to illuminate the body. It is the body qualified in this way, and sometimes called by Plotinus 'the conjoint', that is the bearer of powers such as sense-perception, growth and nutrition. Memory and discursive reason are a little different since they may operate both through, and independently of, the physical body. Where then does he locate the individual person? Since it is 'we' who perceive, he locates the 'we' or self at the level of discursive reason, which is above, but connected to, the 'conjoint'.[2] For it is reason which eventually processes sense-perceptions.

We should note that there are still some basic cognitive functions below the level of reason and even of sense-perception. Although sense-perception ceases when the soul is separated from the body at death and is thus not a part of the higher soul where the 'we' operates, the faculty of sense-perception nevertheless contains a certain element of judgement, which may be exercised before a perception has been transmitted to discursive reason. Similarly there are certain memories which do not survive after death but are stored in a faculty of *phantasia* which is part of the lower soul. Because Plotinus is concerned to show that the soul is something incorporeal and cannot be affected by the corporeal, he takes a great interest in analysing the process of sense-perception in order to explain just how a transmission from outside can take place without the incorporeal power of soul being affected. One of the most interesting of his observations is his distinction between sensation and perception. We may receive a stimulus without actually perceiving it. Perception is not of the thing outside, the object of perception, but of its image received by the living being. But these images or impressions are not physical impressions like that of a signet ring on wax (he is thinking here of Stoic theory) but are incorporeal and 'intelligible'.

> So external perception is the image of this perception of the soul, which is in its essence truer and is a contemplation of forms alone without being affected.[3]

So here perception which deals with the external (sensation) is distinguished from perception proper which belongs to the soul and operates internally without contact with the physical object, and therefore is not directly affected by the external object. It is from these forms or impressions that the soul develops concepts (with the help of transcendent forms, as we will see).

Discursive reason

Reason, which stands midway between sense-perception and intellection, receives information from both sources. Its own mode of cognition is one of transition as it passes from one thought to another in a chain of arguments, something which is best seen from a comparison with intellect:

> Its knowing is not by search but by possession, its blessedness inherent, not acquired; for all belongs to it eternally and it holds the real eternity imitated by time which, circling round the soul, makes towards the new thing and passes by the old. Soul deals with thing after thing – now Socrates; now a horse.[4]

Discursive reason has its knowledge from elsewhere (from the perception of the physical universe, but primarily from intellect). Yet what it sees are only images which are a more evolved or unfolded expression of what is in intellect.[5] Equally, though of less importance, it does not have direct contact with physical objects but deals with images of them too. It is also characterised by process as it passes from one object to another or moves through the stages of an argument. It is not eternal in the sense of being in a timeless condition. But, as we will learn later,[6] reason does not necessarily operate *in* time. For reason can operate outside the physical body, for example after death when the soul is separated from the physical realm. And while the realm of Soul is not eternity, Soul is not in time either: rather it is time, as being the cause of time. This suggests that the process involved in reasoning is one of logical rather than chronological ordering, or of thinking of a part rather than of the whole. It may help to clarify this notion if we realise that for Plotinus there is another mode of reasoning which seems to apply only to human beings and not to universal Soul. This is deliberation or calculation (*logismos*), which involves detailed planning and concern with specific parts within the physical world and, therefore, in time.

Reason and intellect

But each of us has a higher level of activity, intellect, which, though totally independent of body, is necessary for the interpretation of our perceptions of the physical world. The intellect provides essential information to the individual in the embodied state for the operations of discursive reason. Information, Plotinus argues, comes to reason from two sources: from sense-perception from below, as it were, and from intellect, which is above. In interpreting the world around us the two sources are combined. So, for example, if we make the judgement that Socrates is good, we see Socrates with our eyes and note his behaviour, but make the particular judgement that he is good by appealing to our knowledge of the Good in itself, the absolute standard:

> and if it says whether he is good, its remark originates in what it knows through sense-perception, but what it says about this it has already from itself, since it has a norm of the good in itself.[7]

Our knowledge of the 'good in itself' comes from our intellect to our discursive reason, where it can be deployed to interpret the sense-perception. The distinction of discursive and intuitive reason has its origins both in Plato's distinction of opinion (*doxa*) and true knowledge (*episteme*) and in Aristotle's concept of intellect. And so Plotinus can argue for the necessity of a level of intellect on Platonic and Aristotelian grounds. From Plato comes the doctrine that we need to possess absolute norms in order to make statements about particulars; and from Aristotle the doctrine of the priority of actuality over potentiality, that if there is a mind that thinks there must be a mind that always thinks as its cause:

> Since, then, there exists soul which reasons about what is right and good, and discursive reasoning which enquires about the rightness and goodness of this or that particular thing, there must be some further permanent rightness from which arises the discursive reasoning in the realm of soul. Or how else would it manage to reason? And if soul sometimes reasons about the right and good and sometimes does not, there must be in us intellect which does not reason discursively but always possesses the right.[8]

The same Aristotelian argument is used against the Stoics who believed in the progressive growth of the rational faculties from childhood. For Plotinus intellect is with us from the beginning.[9] It is not, he argues, soul that generates intellect, as the Stoics maintain, but quite the reverse: for the potential could not become actual unless there exists a prior actuality, i.e. the intermittent and imperfect operations of discursive reason can only come about if there is a prior, ever-active and perfect cause, which is what we call intellect.

But intellect has a more fundamental relationship to the soul, for it is the cause of its existence in the first place. This will be more clearly seen when we come to discuss the universal Intellect, but it is equally true of the individual.

The ascent to intellect

The question quite naturally arises why we are not, in fact, permanently aware of such absolute values or, in a larger sense, of the workings of our own intellect. The reality is that some people are hardly ever or never aware of them. Plotinus' frequent response to this question is to claim that we direct our attention either outwards towards sense-perception or inwards towards our intellect. The needs of the body and the affairs of everyday life attract us towards an outward deployment of our attention. The task of the philosopher is to reduce the effect of such distractions to the minimum and to train himself to 'keep the soul's power of apprehension pure and ready to hear the voices from on high'.[10] What is meant by 'we' in this context and what faculty it employs are questions frequently raised by Plotinus. Two major issues immediately present themselves as problematical. There is, first, the traditional Platonic view of the soul as being both transcendent and immanent. How can the soul both be engaged in the world and yet separate itself off from the body in order to think clearly? Are these alternative states or can they occur at the same time and, if so, at which level or state are we to locate the self? And, second, there seem to be different modes of reasoning: for example deliberation and a higher kind of reasoning. Sometimes Plotinus presents a very clear and schematic account of the role of discursive reason which, he argues, plays a medial role between a transcendent intellect and those powers of the soul more directly related to the body, such as sense-perception, alluded to earlier. At other times, when he tries to elucidate the differing roles of reason, his analysis is more subtle and complex. These accounts need not, however, be inconsistent. At the end of the searching treatise on 'What is the living being?' he can still conclude that the 'we' doing the present philosophical investigation (discursive reason) is our higher soul which, though it can be said to be intellectual and act intellectually, is not to be identified with intellect:

> And intellectual activity is ours in the sense that the soul is intellectual and intellectual activity is its higher life, both when the soul operates intellectually and when intellect acts upon us. For intellect, too, is a part of ourselves and to it we ascend.[11]

Another treatise (V.3), written not long before, helps to explain a little more the relationship of reason to intellect. The context is self-knowledge. How, he asks, does the soul know itself? It can know itself in the sense of being aware of bodily functions, which are part of our being. But it knows these as something other than itself. It knows intelligibles too, but as impressions and as though from outside itself. The reasoning faculty, which processes impressions from below and from above, appears to be the centre of our being, of what we are. We are, he says 'the principal part of the soul, in the middle between two powers, a worse and a better, the worse that of sense-perception, the better that of intellect' (V.3.3, 38–40). We are aware, he claims, of a higher faculty, the intellect, which somehow transcends us, is our 'king', as it were, while sense-perception is our 'messenger'. But there is a way in which we can identify with this higher faculty. Although Plotinus here clearly locates the centre of human consciousness, what he often calls the 'we', at the level of discursive reason, he is, nevertheless, strongly drawn to finding a special role for intellect as the very core of the real self – intellect is in some way 'ours'. At the level of discursive reason, 'knowing oneself' extends only as far as knowing one's object, the self, as other and therefore merely an image of oneself. Only at the level of intellect are thinker and object (the self) one. Thus the soul has only an image of the self and the world of real being, i.e. intellect. And although we too are ultimately rooted in some way in Intellect our self-knowledge is so far only an image knowledge. Yet it is possible to go further in the discovery of self. At the very highest level we somehow transcend our empirical self and cross over to the level of intellect:

> The man who knows himself is double, one knowing the nature of the reasoning which belongs to the soul, and one up above this man, who knows himself according to intellect because he has become that intellect; and by that intellect he thinks himself again, not any longer as man, but having become altogether other.[12]

Plotinus here has effectively burst the bounds of the ontological framework in which the individual, the 'we', has so far been contained, for the 'we' has so far been identified with a certain level of reality, discursive reason. But what, we may ask, has crossed over and *become* intellect? It cannot be that our discursive reason has itself become intellect and thus ceased to be discursive reason and the centre of our normal conscious life. We, as 'man', have not ceased to exist. What has happened here is that the straightforward account which locates the self in discursive reason, where reason is faced with the stark alternative of receiving either from above or from below, is for Plotinus no longer sufficient. For true, as opposed to image knowledge, to take place, the knower must be on the same level, even identical, with what is known. The 'we' which passes over to 'become' this self-knower eludes the strict categories of being expressed as levels of reality, either as soul or as intellect. It is a sort of floating barometer of the self which determines the level of reality that is to play the leading role in our own spiritual well-being. Thus, in these chapters, Plotinus moves from one model of self-discovery to another. He starts with a self-discovery and return to intellect which relies on a notion of external consciousness. We, the empirical self, located at the level of discursive reason, may or may not be conscious of our intellect. The distractions of sense-perception may cause our attention to turn outwards. He concludes, however, with a theory which overrides the limitations of this analysis.

Elsewhere Plotinus has some interesting observations about consciousness which help to throw more light on this more fluid concept of the self. We may refer back to what we have already said about the distinction made by Plotinus between sensation and perception. In a treatise written about the same time as V.3 he observes that the intellect may be active even if we are not conscious of this activity. Our central faculty is like a mirror which receives images from above or from below. If the mirror is disturbed by images from below, or broken, it no longer reflects the higher images. He then goes on to observe that in our everyday life we perform many activities, both practical and theoretical, without being fully aware of them. A reader, for example, may not be aware that he is reading. Moreover, he adds, conscious awareness may even impair such activities (I.4.10). These observations are intended to help us to understand that in the midst of the most extreme physical predicaments and human disasters the good man can meaningfully be said to be happy. If he has lost his entire family in war, is overcome with illness or, most extreme of all, if he suffers the most excruciating of tortures, roasted alive in the bronze bull invented by Phalaris, the tyrant of Acragas, he can still be said to be happy. The main point to be noted is that when he is in the bull of Phalaris he is not aware of the activity of his intellect; but this does not mean that this activity of intellectual self-knowledge is not taking place: its taking place is independent of his awareness of it. An interesting corollary necessarily follows: the man in the bull of Phalaris is aware of being tortured; but it is his empirical self which is aware of this, while the higher self is inward turned in contemplation and unaffected. For self-knowledge at the level of intellect is also a level of awareness, but of a fuller kind, since this awareness or consiousness is characterised by the unity of subject and object. Such a unity is something not achieved in normal empirical awareness which is of an image only. Plotinus thus believes that he can offer a much more meaningful explanation of the well-being of the good man in extreme situations than that offered, for example, by the Stoics, for his is grounded in the clear distinction of two levels of consciousness, each vested in a different level of reality: on the one hand empirical consciousness vested in the discursive reason of the soul, on the other the level of true knowledge and, therefore, of perfect self-consciousness, vested in the individual intellect:

> But the 'greatest study' is always ready to hand and always with him, all the more if he is in the so-called 'bull of Phalaris' which it is silly to call pleasant, though people keep on saying that it is; for according to their philosophy that which says that its state is pleasant is the very same thing that is in pain; according to ours that which suffers pain is one thing and there is another which even while it is compelled to accompany that which suffers pain remains in its own company and will not fall short of the vision of the universal good.[13]

Of course all intellects by their very nature are always active (rather than potential). In this sense it is not simply the activity of the good man's intellect that distinguishes his life from that of the average person or the bad man. The difference must lie in that crossing over or 'becoming' intellect which we discussed above. There is a moment in the life of the good man when he reaches up to and attains the level of the life of intellect which then becomes the dominant focal point of his existence. Such an achievement comes only after a sustained effort of rational enquiry built on a life of moral virtue. It is in this sense that the good man's life is like that of a lantern which maintains its light even in the midst of a storm:

> His light burns within, like the light in a lantern when it is blowing hard outside with a great fury of wind and storm.[14]

Intellect itself

When we turn to examine intellect in itself rather than its relationship to discursive reason and sense-perception we can identify two important functions. It acts as the level of true knowledge and it is also often identified with our true inner self. True knowledge occurs when the thinking subject, intellect, is identical with the object of thought, the intelligible, in the act of intellection, i.e. when thinker, object and act are one. The concept of knowledge as identity of the act of thinking and thought object is suggested already in Aristotle's statement that 'contemplative knowledge is the same as what is so known'.[15] Certainly, for Plotinus, this idea was linked with Aristotle's notion that god is his own thoughts – 'the divine thought and its object will be the same'.[16] Plotinus' use of this Aristotelian concept may have been prompted by the arguments of the Sceptics against the validity of sense-perception in which they exploited the difference between the object perceived and the perception as image of the external object. Thus we never have direct knowledge of the thing itself but only of its representation or image.[17] Plotinus explicitly contrasts sense-perception and knowledge. The latter is no longer the apprehension of an image but of the thing itself because there is no gap between them to be bridged; the knower is the object known. But 'that which is known by sense-perception is an image of the thing, and sense-perception does not apprehend the thing itself: for that remains outside'.[18] Such a theory was novel and Longinus, the official head of the Academy in Athens, argued strongly against it and in support of what he took to be the normal Platonic view that the mind contemplates the Forms as existing outside itself. He encouraged his former student Porphyry, who was now studying with Plotinus in Rome, to oppose the theory that the objects of thought are not outside the intellect. Despite initial opposition Porphyry was eventually convinced that true knowledge could be maintained only on the basis of Plotinus' theory. Plotinus' conviction derives largely from the notion of 'image' and the strict distinction between an object and its image. Even at the level of abstract thought our reason, according to Plotinus, deals with images, both of physical realities and of eternal truths, the equivalent of the Platonic Forms. If intellect is a cognitive faculty which can know fully and unerringly then it is necessary that it contemplates its objects not as images, not as other than itself; therefore it must *be* its objects.

> If one grants that the objects of thought are as completely as possible outside intellect, and that intellect contemplates them as absolutely outside it, then it cannot possess the truth of them and must be deceived in everything it contemplates. For they would be the true realities; and on this supposition it will contemplate them without

> possessing them, but will only get images of them in a knowledge of this sort.[19]

The argument is essentially a negative one, moving from the denial of an insufficient account of knowledge to the assertion of the basic requirements of an adequate account. But this is only the beginning of the enquiry since Plotinus returns again and again to elucidate the meaning of the doctrine of the identity of knower and known. A particularly close analysis may be found in his treatise *On the Knowing Hypostases*,[20] a treatise which we have already cited in connection with man's ascent from discursive reason to intellect. The context of this treatise is different from that of V.5 in that the concern is not with knowing the physical world or the world of Forms, but with knowing oneself. Thus here the object of the knower is himself. The first part of this treatise is a metaphysical expression of the Delphic injunction to 'know thyself'. In fact it will turn out that our 'self' is the intelligibles; but we can leave this aside for the moment to concentrate on the way in which he tries to elucidate the notion of self-knowledge in chapters 5 and 6.

Plotinus sometimes suggests that there is some even higher element of the individual beyond intellect.

> And if soul sometimes reasons about the right and good and sometimes does not, there must be in us intellect which does not reason discursively but always possesses the right, and there must be also the principle and cause and God of Intellect.[21]

He goes on to explain that the One acts as the centre for all individuals, like the radii of a circle which share a common centre. The conviction that we possess such a capacity comes from his own experience of mystical union with a reality more lofty than Intellect: the ultimate principle of everything, the One. Such experience was for him as self-evident as his perception of the physical universe or of the rational workings of the mind. In a sense it was more real insofar as the physical universe and even the soul are lower in the hierarchy of being than intellect and the One, which is above being. For Plotinus the experience of contact with this ultimate principle was a given fact, though not one that was easy to explain or encapsulate in terms of everyday rational discourse. Self-knowledge is the very core of Plotinus' philosophy. All philosophical endeavour commences with a search for the true reality within oneself by the discovery of the different levels of one's own being and it is a search that begins from where we are in this world as individuals possessed of a physical body. This internal search will also reveal the world of objective reality of which we are an integral part. This will become clearer as we now turn to examine the One, Intellect and Soul as macrocosmic principles.

2

THE ONE

Our exposition has so far followed the way in which Plotinus begins with the introspection of the individual as he seeks to find that element in him which searches for reality. The discovery of the different levels of the self ended in the experience of the self as one with the principle of all other selves, the One. This personal exploration is, however, not the only source of knowledge about the structure of the universe. When, in this section, we introduce Plotinus' ideas about the macrocosmic principles of the universe we will concentrate, as he often does, on the universe outside the self and will not only argue from the bottom upwards, i.e. from the physical universe as presented to sense-perception, but also from the first principle downwards, since Plotinus presents us with arguments that grapple with the problem first raised by the earliest Greek philosophers: how did this world of variety and multiplicity derive from an original unity. Of course that problem which was handed on to all subsequent Greek philosophers was itself bound up with the more ultimate unstated conviction that all things in some way do form a unity, that the intelligibility, even the existence of the physical cosmos is dependent on its coherence as a unity.

Plotinus, and even more so subsequent Neoplatonists such as Proclus,[1] pursued this expression of unity in a much more radical way than Plato, Aristotle or most of his immediate predecessors. Of course, he found in Plato the suggestion of his own doctrine of an ultimate principle of unity, in the sun analogy and the Form of the Good in the *Republic* and, more intricately, in the arguments of the *Parmenides*. Plato's explorations, in this dialogue, of the relationship of the verb *is* and its subject *it* or *one* were interpreted by Plotinus in a metaphysical sense to yield a series of concepts which provided a One beyond Being (as in the *Republic*). But the insistence on the utter otherness of the first principle is radical, however much its roots may be found in the tradition of Greek philosophy. Moreover this search for a solution to the problem of unity first raised by the Presocratics is conducted by Plotinus at every niveau of his metaphysical system since each level, beginning from the lowest, displays an increasing degree of unity and presents the problem of reconciling unity and plurality in increasingly concentrated form. For all these reasons it is appropriate to begin our exposition with the One.

The One

Plotinus argues that it is necessary that there is such a thing as an absolute One since without it individual entities could not exist. Since they do there must be a One.

> It is by the One that all beings are beings, both those which are primarily beings and those which are in some way classed among beings. For what could exist if it was not one? If beings are deprived of what we call unity they do not exist. An army, a choir, or a flock do not exist if they are not one; and even a house or a ship does not exist if it has not unity, for a house is one and so is a ship, and if it loses its unity the house is no longer a house or the ship a ship.[2]

Beginning from the lowest, each level of reality is examined for the unity which it displays. As we ascend from physical objects to soul and then to intellect we will find an increasing level of unity, but none of these levels is identical with unity itself, rather they have the quality of unity as something other than what they are themselves. Each of these levels is a plurality as well as a unity. Plotinus' argument here is that there must be a unifying cause at each level distinct from that which is unified. And so when we come to the highest level of unity, Intellect, there must be a cause beyond it which causes its unity. The principle that there must be a prior simple cause, as it is espoused by Plotinus, goes beyond the notion that things are composed of unities to ask what has made each of these components one. This can only be a transcendent cause which is above all instances of unity.

> There can be no many if there is not a one from which or in which these are, or in general a one, and a one which is

> counted first before the others, which must be taken alone, itself by itself.[3]

He then goes on to reject as inadequate the notion that unity can be explained simply from what is immanent within the unified; we must posit a source of unity which is above the unified:

> But if it was together with the others, since it was taken with the others but all the same was different from the others, we should have to reject it because it was with the others, and look for what underlies the others and is no longer with the others, but itself by itself.[4]

In a way this is the ultimate solution to the 'third man' criticism of the Platonic Forms. The transcendent One is the ultimate cause of the relationship between the unity and plurality of Intellect, providing each component with its coherent and unified identity and at the same time securing the unity of their relationships to each other as a whole. Intellect, despite its unity of subject and object, is still a plurality, a one-many. Neoplatonism's distinct contribution to metaphysics is to recognise this plurality and to posit as its unifier a cause which transcends Intellect.

The One is unknowable

This ultimate principle of unity, the One, cannot strictly be named or spoken about at all; for this would compromise its status. Any statement made about it will necessarily be composed of a subject and predicate, which already implies a duality. But, as we have seen, Plotinus has a good deal to say about the One. There are a number of ways in which it is possible to gain some insight into the nature of the One and thus to say something about it, as long as we realise that any statements made about it, even the most basic that it is the ultimate cause of all things, are in the end relative to us rather than to it and thus do not limit it in any way. Tradition, experience and reason all provide approaches. The philosophical tradition and, of course Plato above all, teaches us that there is an ultimate unity. Most directly of all, the One may be reached and experienced by the individual, though only after the appropriate moral and intellectual preparation. But this experience, which we will describe later when we talk of Plotinus' mysticism,[5] is not to be equated in any way with normal conscious or discursive experience. It is above even intuitive thought. When we afterwards recall this direct contact with the One we can use only the thoughts and language of a lower level of experience in order to describe it. And in doing so we are not strictly describing it but only pointing towards it. What is, however, important to note here is that Plotinus does think that it is worth the effort to attempt such a description. For Plotinus is all the time pushing forward the boundaries of what it is possible to know and doing so with the only means known to the philosopher, the use of discursive reason. The attempt to describe the experience of the One is not the only approach that reason can offer. We can employ negative statements, analogy and inferences from a lower level of reality.[6] Saying what the One is not was a method later adopted by Christian theologians as negative or apophatic theology. The argument from what is produced by the One we have already partly seen in the observation of unity in the physical world. Since Intellect is the first product of the One and therefore the nearest to it, it can provide the most precise indicator of the One's nature by its own manifestation of unity: that of thinker and object of thought. The use of analogy requires further comment. One of the most enlivening features of Plotinus' style of philosophical exposition is his use of metaphors. But we must be careful to avoid the negative judgement of these as pure ornamentation, or worse, as dangerously loose talk. We have already seen an example of how Plotinus is careful sometimes to correct a metaphor by qualification or by the addition of a further metaphor or analogy. More strictly, his use of metaphor is often rooted in analogy. For Plotinus an analogy is not always simply an illustration from another aspect of reality, but rather from another level of reality. And since each level of reality depends on that above it, there is a metaphysical and causal connection which, it can be argued, could point to some similarity between caused and cause. Plotinus never explicitly enunciates a theory of analogy although in I.2.1 when discussing virtue he notes the non-reciprocal nature of some types of likeness, where the cause does not necessarily display all the features of the caused. For example, it is only in the physical house that we find measured proportion, ordering and arrangement of parts. The intelligible house, being unextended in space, does not possess these aspects. But it is clear that a theory is at least implied and is sometimes seen in operation, for example in the case of the various analogies applied to intellect.

As principle of all it must be all-powerful

The question now arises how plurality or anything at all could derive from pure unity, the One. The One produces of necessity because it is perfect. This necessity is not one of compulsion, but comes from the nature of the One itself and its own perfection. A number of fundamental principles are brought into play at this point. Plotinus takes from the Aristotelian tradition the idea that everything which reaches its maturity (which is equivalent to its perfection) produces an offspring. In fact it must produce something, if it is perfect.[7]

> And all things when they come to perfection produce; the One is always perfect and therefore produces everlastingly; and its product is less than itself.[8]

And here the further elaboration is added that what it produces must be inferior to the producer. This too is probably based on biological facts: a man produces a child, and the child, since it is not yet a mature adult, is inferior to its producer. Plotinus also argues for the principle on the grounds that the actual (and therefore perfect) is prior to the potential, which, since it has not yet become what it is going to be, is less perfect than what has already achieved its potentiality. This also accounts for the fact that the producer does not have to be the same as the produced. The fact that Intellect is produced by the One does not mean that the One is an Intellect.

> Now there is no necessity for anyone to have what he gives, but in this kind of situation one must consider that the giver is greater, and that what is given is less than the giver; for that is how coming to be is among the real beings. For that which is actual must be first, and those that come after must be potentially those before them.[9]

Another approach to the latter is to argue that if the first principle produced another principle identical with itself, this would then itself be the One. But the One is unique, therefore what comes after the One is less than the One.[10]

Plotinus does, however, sometimes suggest that what is produced from the One is in some sense prefigured in the One or present in it in a seminal way. After arguing that the products of the One derive from the One as cause of their continued existence, he presses the analysis further to assert that the One somehow possesses them:

> But how is that One the principle of all things? Is it because as principle it keeps them in being, making each one of them exist? Yes, and because it brought them into existence. But how did it do so? By possessing them beforehand. But it has been said that in this way it will be a multiplicity. But it had them in such a way as not to be distinct: they are distinguished on the second level.[11]

In his attempt to answer this final question he can also say that the One is all things in a transcendent way[12] or, more challengingly, he sometimes allows that the One has an 'activity' of its own which on one occasion he even calls 'thinking'. But he then goes on to qualify this statement; for the 'thinking' ascribed to the One does not imply that the One itself 'thinks' or is a 'thinker', but rather that it acts as the cause of thinking in another, namely Intellect: and thus in the final analysis it is Intellect that really is the 'thinker':

> We must not put him [the One] on the level of the thinker, but rather on that of thinking (*noesis*). But thinking does not think, but is a cause of thinking to another; and the cause is not the same as the caused.[13]

Although the required utter simplicity of the One is probably best served by the way of negation, the ascription of positive characteristics is not the polar opposite of negation since the intention of the way of negation is not to remove all qualities from the ultimate principle but rather to suggest that it transcends them. To declare that one cannot ascribe being to it is not to deny that it exists. Rather it 'is' in a sense greater than that expressed by the verb 'is', which even in its most basic utterance requires a subject; and to say 'it is' suggests two concepts, the subject and its activity/essence, and therefore a duality.[14] Strictly speaking one cannot even say that the One is the cause of everything. It is only in our relation to it that we can speak of cause. But the ascription of positive characteristics may be seen as a way of suggesting in what way it is not like and transcends everything else.

Emanation

One modern way of describing Plotinus' explanation for the derivation of principles from each other is to speak of a theory of emanation. The concept of emanation ascribed to Plotinus is based partly on stressing the analogies he employs, but it tends to limit and distort the subtleties of Plotinus' exposition. Although he often uses the analogy of a spring of water flowing forth, the image is consciously modified and corrected.

> Think of a spring which has no other origin, but gives the whole of itself to rivers, and is not used up by the rivers but remains itself at rest ... or the life of a huge plant, which goes through the whole of it while its origin remains and is not dispersed over the whole, since it is, as it were, firmly settled in the root. So this origin gives to the plant its whole life in its multiplicity, but remains itself not multiple but the origin of the multiple life.[15]

Here the image of the spring is modified not only within itself – we are to imagine it as remaining undiminished – but also by the application of another image, that of the life of a plant. Finally and more technically the source is to be termed the 'origin' (*arche*) which is not multiple in itself. But frequently Plotinus employs a more precise analysis of this moment of production. Drawing on an observation from the physical world, which is applied as an analogy to the incorporeal, he notes that many things, both living and apparently inanimate, demonstrate a twofold activity, an activity *of* their essence, that which makes them what they are, and an activity *from* their essence, an activity which is caused by the inner essential activity and which carries its effect outwards beyond the object.

> In each and every thing there is an activity which belongs to substance and one which goes out from substance; and that which belongs to substance is the active actuality which is each particular thing, and the other activity derives from that first one, and must in everything be a consequence of it, different from the thing itself: as in fire there is a heat which is the content of its substance, and another which comes into being from that primary heat when fire exercises the activity which is native to its substance in abiding unchanged as fire. So it is in the higher world; and much

> more so there, while the Principle abides 'in its own proper way of life',[16] the activity generated from the perfection in it and its coexistent activity acquires substantial existence, since it comes from a great power, the greatest indeed of all, and arrives at being and substance; for that Principle is 'beyond being'.[17]

We shall see later how central to Plotinus' metaphysics of Intellect is the idea that a substance must be identical with its own actuality if it is to be perfectly what it is.

The One as cause

In the passage above we note that in the case of the One, that which is 'beyond being', its outer activity is not quite identical with the next level of reality, Intellect or Being. The outer activity is said to 'acquire' substantial existence and to 'arrive at being and substance'. Now when we consider the One as productive of a power outside itself we can speak of it in terms of *efficient* causality. This external power, as befits the One, reflects the unbounded and infinite power of the One itself: it is 'indefinite'. Plotinus frequently connects this concept with the Pythagorean concept of the indefinite Dyad. This idea, taken up by Platonists, was a metaphysical expression of the Pythagorean column of opposites. The most important of these for cosmogony was the pair 'odd and even' or one and two, the unit providing limit and form, the 'even' or two providing the indefinite base which is to receive form. For Plotinus this reception of limit is not altogether passive but comes from the product of the One which, in Plotinus' terminology, is said to turn back upon the One. Thus the production of Intellect, and of the other levels of reality, is not merely a one-way process of efficient causality from above, but involves the latent power at each level, which naturally strives for perfection and completion by turning to what is above it. In this sense the One acts as *final* cause and demonstrates its nature as the Good, that to which all strive. Plotinus exploits the Platonic expression of this idea from the *Symposium* when, in his treatise on Beauty, he identifies this propensity to strive for the Beautiful and the Good with the power of love. There are also, of course, affinities with Aristotle's unmoved mover who acts by drawing things towards him as a loved person does.[18] But although Plotinus distinguishes with precision the different elements in this movement of procession from, and return to, the One, he is also careful to correct the impression that this is a process. For there can be no process in the eternal sphere, rather must we point to significant aspects which we identify as moments since we must apply the limiting categories of time which are an essential feature of discursive thought.[19] This 'self-correction' may be seen at the end of the following exposition of the 'process' in which Intellect is formed.

> This, when it has come into being, turns back upon the One and is filled, and becomes Intellect by looking towards it. Its halt and turning towards the One constitutes being, its gaze upon the One, Intellect. Since it halts and turns upwards towards the One that it may see, it becomes *at once* Intellect and being.[20]

The apparently discrete moments of halting, turning upwards and seeing are in fact simultaneous (*at once*) or more accurately timeless. This passage also suggests a further way in which the One affects what it produces, or rather, in which that which it produces is influenced by the One. For here what is produced is said to 'look' at the One. This contemplation of the One results in the enforming of the One's product so that it becomes Intellect. Thus the One also acts in some way as a *formal* cause.

Although he affirms that it is strictly indescribable and unknowable even to intellectual apprehension, Plotinus nevertheless perseveres in stating and exploring the necessary role of the One as ultimate metaphysical principle. The transcendent One is probably the most characteristic feature of Neoplatonism, but Plotinus did not have the last word, as we will see when we look at later developments, on the difficult issue of the nature of the ultimate principle and its relationship to its products.

3

INTELLECT

Although the One is the ultimate principle and source of all, Intellect stands at the very core of Plotinus' metaphysics. The Greek term *Nous* defies exact translation into English. The German *Geist* gives a more rounded impression than the English 'mind' or 'intellect' which suggest more the notion of discursive reason, which Plotinus locates at a lower level than the intuitive thought characteristic of what we will translate as 'Intellect'. But Intellect is not simply an activity, it is a real existent; in fact it is Being par excellence. This combination of Thought and Being derives from Plotinus' deep consideration of vital elements of Aristotelian metaphysics which he deployed in his interpretation of Plato. Put at its very simplest he has creatively combined the Aristotelian idea of a self-contemplating deity with the Platonic Forms. Such a combination was not entirely new. Plato had posited the Forms, or ideal archetypes, as the ultimate source of all knowledge and reality; while Aristotle, finding problems with this theory, not least with its static nature, preferred to place a divine intellect as the first cause. Subsequent Platonists sought ways of utilising both of these concepts. The idea of the Forms as the thoughts of God had a long history before Plotinus, as had the general influence on Platonism of Aristotelian ideas. What is new in Plotinus is the vigorously systematic and radical way in which he manages these ideas to achieve a richly coherent concept of an active intelligible cosmos. The static Platonic world of Forms is transformed into a vital level of Being.

We will begin by examining Plotinus' reasons for asserting the existence of a level of reality which he calls Intellect. He argues both downwards from the necessity of the One to produce a lower level of reality which has the characteristics of Intellect, and upwards from the physical universe and soul, both of which point to some higher principle as the cause of their existence. We have seen that the One must produce something; but why should it produce an Intellect? An appeal can be made to the common philosophical tradition which envisages a divine mind of some kind as the highest principle;[1] since for Plotinus the One has usurped this role, Intellect can be put on the next level as its closest image just as light is the image of the sun.[2] Plotinus regards this as an important and difficult question, since it requires us to explain not only how plurality can emerge from absolute unity but also why this first manifestation of plurality should have the characteristics which are associated with thinking.

Seen from this world a number of observations serve to demonstrate the need for archetypes both for the objects we see around us and for the activity of cognition in general. The world itself consists of both natural things and artefacts. Both categories are a combination of matter and form. What, then, is the origin of their forms if not some transcendent source?[3] Soul too, which thinks and gives life, is also a sort of compound and receives these qualities from elsewhere. In fact the whole universe must have form given to it from a transcendent source which is a sort of 'intelligible cosmos'.[4] This enforming process has two aspects: there are the Forms or, as Plotinus prefers to call them, the 'rational principles', which are similar to Platonic Forms or archetypes of objects, and there is also the activity of enforming, of the agent, whether World Soul or ultimately Intellect, which 'gives' the Forms.[5] This crucial observation is another example of Plotinus' concern to combine the 'static' and dynamic in his interpretation of the Platonic theory of Forms. Where these two aspects are finally reconciled is in Intellect, which not only has the Forms and is a thinking and therefore productive being, but where the Forms are identical with the activity of thinking.

Another argument from the lower to the higher may be found in Plotinus' analysis of the inadequacy of soul, which we have mentioned in chapter 1,[6] where we pointed out the application of the Aristotelian concept of the priority of actuality to potentiality: if there is discursive reason, the characteristic activity of soul, there must, of necessity, be a higher form of cognition which is eternally active and can thus act as the cause and source of discursive reasoning. The name we give to this form of cognition is 'intellect', in which essence and activity are identical. This concept of actuality becomes crucial in Plotinus' account of Intellect, as we will see.

The nature of Intellect

Intellect as an 'intelligible cosmos' is both the Forms, the true Being of Plato, and an active agent, a thinker. In this way it can be identified with the 'living being' and demiurge of Plato's *Timaeus*.[7] Earlier Platonists and Plotinus' contemporary, Longinus, who was the official head of the Academy in Athens, may have regarded the Forms as the thoughts of the divine mind, but they did not take the final step of completely identifying the two. It was a thesis which Plotinus had to defend vigorously. And yet the elucidation and articulation of the relationship of these aspects within Intellect stands as one of the most important of Plotinus' philosophical achievements and one which provided subsequent philosophers and theologians with the conceptual framework to explore ways of expressing the working of the divine nature. There is a further sense in which it may be regarded as one of the most sophisticated attempts to resolve the relationship of one and many. The reconciliation of this pair might be seen as one of the major inherited problems of Greek philosophy and it is nowhere more central than in Neoplatonism, a strictly monist system which must account for plurality. Unity and plurality are reconciled in different degrees at all levels of the Neoplatonic system and nowhere with greater ingenuity than at the level of Intellect.

'Everything together'

Intellect is at once a plurality and a unity: it is a one-many. Using a phrase of Anaxagoras which Plotinus is fond of quoting, it is 'everything together', and thus the source of all things, i.e. all the Forms, which are each distinct and yet form a unity. This provides a basic solution to the difficult problem that Plato faced in tackling the relationship of Forms to each other. All the Forms or Intelligibles are at once a plurality and distinct, yet equally a unity as Being. In addition, Intellect brings together and yet keeps separate the two ideas of Being/Form and the Intellect which thinks them: they too are one and yet distinct. How can the Intelligibles be both one and many? Plotinus presents a possible solution by pointing to the way in which, even at the level of the individual soul, we can possess many ideas together without these ideas being confused. Surely then at a level of cognition, which is beyond that of the discursive reasoning of soul, we can expect a higher level of integration. This observation is expanded by a number of analogies. This unity in plurality is compared to the way in which a genus includes its species or that in which a seed somehow contains within it the 'parts' which will subsequently emerge and become manifest in the creature when born:

> The powers of seeds give a likeness of what we are talking about: for all the parts are undistinguished in the whole, and their rational forming principles are as if in one central point; and all the same there is one principle of the eye and another of the hand, known from the sense-object which is produced by it to be distinct.[8]

It is clear here that Plotinus is presenting us with analogies rather than simple metaphors, since both genus and species, and the seed, are real instances, though at a different level, of the principle they are invoked to illustrate. This is particularly clear in the case of the seed: for the united powers of the seed are conceived as immaterial rational principles whose pluralised manifestation lies in their power to create differentiated forms without themselves losing their original unity. The seed exemplifies the power of 'reason principles', or immanent forms, in action. What Plotinus here has in mind is the male sperm (the ovary was at this time thought to be a mere passive receptacle for the sperm) which as a physical medium already contains the powers which are later to become manifest as distinct and visible parts, eyes and hands, in the child when born. A yet more direct and powerfully illustrative instance is contained in the analogy of scientific thought: its separate theorems, Plotinus says, do not make sense without the whole, and thus their power must be seen as a whole, but they can nevertheless be treated as individual components:

> Each individual Idea is not other than Intellect, but each is Intellect. And Intellect as a whole is all the Forms, and each individual Form is an individual intellect, as the whole body of knowledge is all its theorems, but each theorem is a part of the whole, not as being spatially distinct, but as having its particular power in the whole. This Intellect therefore is in itself, and since it possesses itself in peace is everlasting fullness.[9]

Not only is there a unity of Forms and Intellect, and of Forms and Being, but just as Being is Intellect, so also are the individual Beings to be identified with intellects. Thus each Form is an intellect and all Forms together are Intellect.[10]

Actuality and potentiality

Plotinus also surprisingly employs the Aristotelian concepts of actuality and potentiality to help in making coherent the idea of plurality in unity at the level of intellect. I say surprisingly because in his treatise *On Actuality and Potentiality* he quite clearly denies the presence of potentiality in the intelligible world, which is exactly what we would expect.[11] It would seem then that if Plotinus is to be consistent his application of 'potentiality' to the intelligible world must in some sense be analogous. The idea enables him to explain how the particular can be in the universal and at the same time how the immanent particular can be said to be universal.[12] And more especially within the level of intellect how our own intellect can be at the same time our own, all intellects and the universal Intellect.

> And the great Intellect exists by itself, and so do the particular intellects which are in themselves, and again the partial intellects are comprehended in the whole and the whole in the partial: the particular ones are on their own and in another, and that great Intellect is on its own and in those particulars; and all are potentially in that Intellect which is on its own, which is actually all things at once, but potentially each particular separately, and the particular intellects are actually what they are, but potentially the whole.[13]

It is the concept of potentiality which presents the problem; but Plotinus generally applies the term only to the particular and since nearly every example of the application of these twin principles occurs in the context of analogies it seems likely that he intended them to be understood analogously. We must also give due weight to Plotinus' warnings about the limitations of human thought. When Plotinus uses overt paradoxes (e.g. 'intellect is everything together and again not together'[14]) it is not to mystify or affect a grandiose style, but because we must be constantly reminded of the distinctions which our discursive reason applies to the immaterial, so that we do not complacently imagine that we have pinned down the intelligible world. In a sense all talk of the intelligible is by analogy;

and analogies, in the end, cannot directly define the intelligible but only point us towards its nature.

Being and Intellect

The identity of Being and Intellect or, in other terms, of the object of thought and that which thinks, is, as we have already seen, essential for Plotinus' theory of knowledge.[15] Since Intellect is identical with individual intellects the same theory applies to both and it is sometimes unclear whether Plotinus is referring to one or the other, or perhaps to both at the same time. Here too a distinct debt to Aristotle's concept of the divine may be noted. Aristotle had argued that if god's nature is thinking it would be unworthy of it if it had as its object anything other, and therefore of less value, than itself. Therefore god's nature, and thus god himself, is 'a thinking of thinking'.[16] Two features of this conclusion are important for Plotinus: that the divine mind has itself as the object of its thought and, second, that the divine mind or Intellect has as its essential characteristic the activity of thinking, i.e. its essence is 'thinking'.

Despite the emphasis by Plotinus on the identity of Being and Intellect, it is nevertheless inevitable that they must be distinguished, if only because we employ discursive reason in metaphysical discussion and discursive reason separates and analyses, in this case into thinker and thought. For the same reason there will be a tendency to imply that one precedes the other. Although Plotinus himself often expresses himself in this way, he is deeply conscious of the necessity to correct the analysis given by discursive reason. Depending on the context and the particular emphasis of his discussion he can give the impression that Being precedes Intellect or the other way round. In one particular treatise he can say that 'Intellect establishes them (the real beings) in existence'[17] and yet a few lines later that 'they are neither before it (Intellect) nor after it'. Since, in effect, there can be no temporal priority in the Intelligible, this statement is strictly correct. His tendency, however, is to emphasise the 'priority' of Being,[18] in order to establish its objective existence, or rather to remove the misunderstanding we might have if we were to say, in an unqualified way, that thought produces its object; for this statement might suggest to us that the object of thought is something like a figment of the imagination. And this is, of course, one of the concepts strictly excluded by Plato's theory of transcendent Forms. On the other hand to stress too strongly the 'priority' of Being would favour Longinus' objection to identifying the Forms with Intellect and thus, in Plotinus' eyes, endanger the status of Intellect as the source of truth.

Besides the frequent and important reminder that we are not to apply temporal or spatial concepts to the Intelligible, Plotinus attempts to resolve this difficult problem by exploiting the notion of 'activity/actuality' as a linking concept designating an identity in nature of Being and Intellect. In this context neither has priority as both share in, or better are, a common activity which unites them. Being and Intellect are thus to be seen as different aspects or perspectives of the same substantial activity.

> If then Intellect was thought of as preceding Being, we should have to say that Intellect by coming to actuality in its thinking perfected and produced real beings; but since we must think of Being as preceding Intellect, we must assume that the real beings have their place in the thinking subject, and that the actuality of thinking is in the real beings ... But Being is actuality; so both have one actuality, or rather both are one thing. Being and Intellect are therefore one nature.[19]

In a similar way he can use the idea of 'activity' to elucidate the problem of self-knowledge in Intellect.[20] Here the issue is not 'priority' but the reconciliation of sameness and difference (unity and plurality). For thinking to take place at all there must be at least two elements, a thinker and the object of thought; for perfect self-knowledge there must be identity of thinker and thought. Plotinus finds a solution in the concept of activity which at the level of Intellect must be the activity of thinking. Intellect and its object, the Intelligible or Being, are identical because each can be shown to be 'activity'; and if we are referring to the highest level of Being and of Intellect this activity can only be thinking at the highest level; for at this level there can be only one instance of thinking, that which constitutes truth (see V.5). Thus the activity of Intellect and of Being is absolutely identical. Therefore Intellect and Being are one through thinking, and yet they are distinct aspects:

> If then Intellect is activity and its substance is activity, it is one and the same with its activity; but being and the intelligible are also one with activity. All together are one, intellect, intellection, the intelligible.[21]

Here are three moments, one of which provides their unity. This triad was subsequently exploited both by pagan philosophers and by Christian theologians who found in it fruitful material for trinitarian thinking.[22]

But, as the previous arguments show, the concept of activity provided more than simply a metaphysical link between entities or aspects of entities. It was used by Plotinus to explain the nature both of the Intelligible and of Intellect. Intellect is intellect and not discursive reason because its essence is identical with its activity. It is in Aristotelian terms an 'actuality'. Its thinking cannot be potential for then it would be possible for it not to be thinking and it would thus be unthinking and not intellect. The following passage of Aristotle lies behind Plotinus' argument here:

> But if there is something which is capable of moving things or acting on them, but is not actually doing so, there will not necessarily be movement; for that which has a potency need not exercise it. Nothing, then, is gained even if we suppose eternal substances, as the believers in the Forms do, unless there is to be in them some principle which can cause change; nay, even this is not enough, nor is another substance besides the Forms enough; for if it is not to act, there will be no movement. Further, even if it acts, this will not be enough, if its essence is potency; for there will be no eternal movement, since that which is potentially, may possibly not be. There must, then, be such a principle, whose very essence is actuality. Further, then, these substances must be without matter; for they must be eternal, if anything is eternal. Therefore they must be actuality.[23]

While it may be easy to see why Intellect is an activity or actuality, it is more difficult to see why the intelligible should be an activity. Yet this is what Plotinus claims and appears to argue directly, and not simply from the identification of the intelligible with thinking. Rather the reverse is the argument and this identity is demonstrated from the fact that the intelligible:

> Is certainly not a potentiality and not unintellectual either, nor is it without life, nor again are life and thought brought in from outside to something else, as if to a stone or something lifeless.[24]

He can also argue negatively for the life of Intellect by ruling out other possibilities.[25] The Intelligibles are not propositions nor are they separate Forms. In the latter case there would be nothing to unify them. The assumption here is that the unifying factor is their being one and many through activity. Yet again the static world of Plato's Forms is provided with a dynamic element by the introduction of what Plotinus regards as the definitive categories of the intelligible Being stated by Plato in the *Sophist*.[26] Sameness, difference, movement, rest and being are adopted by Plotinus as the exhaustive categories for defining the nature of the intelligible. The appearance of movement, which is allied to difference, enables Plotinus to cite a Platonic source for the dynamism of his Intelligible world. In a vivid phrase he once describes the Intelligible world as 'seething with activity'.[27]

Another context in which the notion of the Intelligible as activity and life is prominent is Plotinus' attempt to solve the question as to whether and how there can be intelligible forms of irrational creatures.[28] The immediate issue is how the intelligible can be the cause of something irrational. In fact Plotinus argues that even man is rational in a way which is less than that of his intelligible archetype.[29] The power of intellect is gradually deployed and weakened in its manifestations, but without the archetype itself being affected. For example, the archetype of a horse is an intellect thinking of horse as an intellect, for if it were to think horse as without intellect, since intellect and thought are identical at this level, intellect would be non-intellectual. In the case of a horse its intellect has not ceased to be intellect, for it remains even for us in this world potentially intelligent, while actually being an irrational physical creature at the level of life to which it has descended. Thus Intellect expresses itself at different levels of its unfolding. This deployment of power is really something continuous:

> It is then like a long life stretched out at length; each part is different from that which comes next in order, but the whole is continuous with itself, but with one part differentiated from another, and the earlier does not perish in the later.[30]

But this procession may also be regarded as a series of steps or stages, each level the image of its prior, as the reason principles which are the expression of Intellect unfold, and the emphasis can be put on the moments of crucial transition, from the One to Intellect, from Intellect to Soul, from Soul to the universe. Indeed for Plotinus all life and activity[31] is a form of thinking on many different levels. We will begin by identifying this activity at the level of Intellect.

How is Intellect produced?

The immediate 'product' of the One is an indefinite power which constitutes itself as Being by halting and as Intellect by turning back in contemplation of the One.[32] It is thus dependent on the One both for its existence in the first place and for the enforming which the One effects when it is contemplated; and also independent in that it stops of itself and turns in contemplation.[33] This balance of dependence and independence or self-constitution was to be developed later by Proclus. Intellect constitutes its own Being and at the same time its Being as Intellect by becoming enformed and limited by the One. For Being to be it must have limit and form.[34] But Intellect is not able to see the One as it is in its wholeness, but breaks it up, as it were, into a multitude of forms while the One itself is formless.[35] In fact it is a necessary condition of the One's productive power that it transcends Intellect in every respect. Any qualification will limit it and thus require us to posit a yet higher principle.

Another way in which this independence is preserved may be seen when Plotinus suggests that the production of Intellect from the One is characterised by a sort of self-assertion on the part of Intellect.

> But beginning as one it did not stay as it began, but, without noticing it, became many, as if heavy, and unrolled itself because it wanted to possess everything – how much better it would have been for it not to want this, for it became the second.[36]

Elsewhere it is said that Intellect has 'dared' to separate itself from the One.[37] This has little to do with the self-assertion (*tolma*) which is found in some gnostic texts where it refers to the way in which the material universe is created as an aberration and an evil entity.[38] When Plotinus uses such apparently negative language about what is derived from the One it has more to do with preserving the pre-eminence of the One than with denigrating its products, for the physical universe itself is ultimately a product of the One and a good, though inadequate, reflection of its source.

This contemplation of the One by Intellect is described in terms of sight. Before its constitution Intellect is like sight which is not actively seeing. In looking at the One it becomes sight seeing:

> It moved to it [the One] not as Intellect but as sight not yet seeing, but came out possessing the multiplicity which that sight itself made; so that it desired one thing, having vaguely in itself a kind of image of it, but came out having grasped something else which it made many in itself.[39]

The analogy with seeing is sometimes drawn in greater detail. Just as the eye needs the medium of light to illuminate the objects of perception, so the One casts light on the objects of thought so that they can become known. Moreover both the eye and Intellect are able to perceive the light itself. For the sake of the analogy Plotinus supposes that the sun is entirely light with no corporeal element. In the case of Intellect its vision must not be of something external. A parallel for this too may be found in physical sight: when we are in darkness or when the eyelids are shut we sometimes experience a light internal in some way to the eye.[40] In the same way Intellect can see the light that is the One,[41] but without any spatial limitation. This activity of auto-constitution is also timeless.

Sometimes Plotinus distinguishes not only between Intellect's contemplation of its own contents (the archetypes of all that is below it) and its contemplation of the One but also between the latter as the contemplation by which it is constituted and a special and more mystical contemplation of the One.

> Intellect also, then, has one power for thinking, by which it looks at the things in itself, and one by which it looks at what transcends it by a direct awareness and reception, by which also before it saw only, and by seeing acquired intellect and is one. And that first looking is the contemplation of Intellect in its right mind, and the other is Intellect in love, when it goes out of its mind 'drunk with nectar';[42] then it falls in love, simplified into happiness by having its fill; and it is better for it to be drunk with a drunkenness like this than to be more respectably sober.[43]

The first sentence describes the normal contemplation of Intellect by which it constituted itself by turning back in contemplation of the One. It is Intellect contemplating 'in its right mind'. But there follows a description of a different kind of relationship in which the contemplation of the One is a kind of drunkenness and is associated with love, that driving force of spiritual ascent which Plotinus has taken primarily from the *Symposium* and which he treats more specifically in I.6 and his treatise *On Love* III.5. He goes on to say that these two modes of Intellect's relationship with the One are separated temporally only by our discursive reason, for Intellect always has this double relationship with the One. Although this special contemplation is ascribed to Intellect the description suggests the personal experience of mystical union. We should, then, recall the details of this passage when we turn to Plotinus' own experience of mysticism. But we should note that there is a sense in which at every stage of Plotinus' system, and this is especially important for the various levels of the individual, there is a contemplation of the higher which is constitutive of the contemplator and a further aspect of contemplation which goes beyond this and which, in the case of the individual, accounts for the progress of the spiritual life.

The contemplation of Intellect and the emergence of Soul

Just as Intellect is produced by the One as a development of its external power so too Intellect's internal activity is accompanied by a corresponding external activity which develops into Soul.

> For when it is active in itself, the products of its activity are the other intellects, but when it acts outside itself, the product is Soul.[44]

The internal activity of Intellect which is productive in this way is intellection, the form of contemplation appropriate to the level of Intellect. Soul too has its own contemplative power which in turn generates a power that constitutes both the ensouled physical universe and ensouled creatures. Thus the power of contemplation at each level is what constitutes the whole Plotinian universe from the One to the physical world and corresponding to these levels of contemplation are the reason principles which are the expressions of this power, whether as intelligibles, forms at the level of soul or immanent forms in matter. Moreover at each level there is a dynamic of what was later termed procession and return, a process of generation of the lower by the higher in which the lower is caused by and proceeds from the higher but then turns back in contemplation of the higher to achieve its own perfection. In all of this the higher 'remains', or is not affected. The power of contemplation which becomes less potent at each descending level finally loses all effectiveness at its very last manifestation at the lowest level of contact between the reason principles and matter where 'nature', the last reflection of Soul, gives shape and form. And since contemplation is the structuring power of the whole universe and Intellect is the source of contemplation we must ourselves strive to activate our own powers of contemplation and integrate ourselves with Intellect.[45]

4

SOUL, THE UNIVERSE AND MATTER

Soul is the entity by means of which the incorporeal comes into effective contact with the corporeal and which lies, as it were, on the borderline of the transcendent and physical universes. It is, in Plotinus' own words, 'amphibious'.[1] Plotinus takes up the challenge of the Platonic concept of soul which entails a tension between the transcendent functions of soul, seen in its essential capacity to think clearly when freed from the constraints of the body, and its function as the giver of life to the body, whether the individual body or the body of the universe. But if the soul is freed entirely from the body, in what sense can it be said to fulfil the latter function? The stress on soul's essential nature as thinking, that is as being truly soul when it returns into itself in contemplation, is maintained by Plotinus even though he locates the level of truly transcendent thought in Intellect. Although, as we shall see, Plotinus does sometimes appear to blur the distinctions between intellect and soul, he sees in the end little difficulty in maintaining the Platonic concept of the transcendent functioning of soul as a distinct activity of soul as opposed to bodily perception on the one hand and the activities of intellect on the other. The presence of the soul to the body, however, occasions him far greater philosophical difficulties. In his *Life of Plotinus* Porphyry tells us how he raised this difficult issue with Plotinus who then, much to the annoyance of many members of his seminar who were apparently content with straightforward expositions of his thought, declared that the discussion must continue until all of Porphyry's problems and objections had been answered.[2] It is a good example of Plotinus' genuinely thorough, exploratory and questioning style of philosophising. In the case of soul it prompted not only the sort of problem solving in the long treatise (later divided by Porphyry) on 'Problems of the soul'[3] but also the even more fundamental posing of the problem of how the incorporeal is present to the corporeal in *Enneads* VI. 4 and 5. An essential feature of soul, as being incorporeal, is that it is undivided and one. Thus Plotinus can talk about Soul as a whole, whereas we would more naturally begin from a consideration of individual souls. Plotinus must, however, accept the unity of soul, which must then be reconciled with the concept of individual souls. Equally curious for us, but not for him, was the idea that the world has its own soul, responsible for its shaping and life. For Plotinus individual souls and the World Soul are subordinate aspects of Soul as a whole. As embodied individuals we are closely related to the World Soul which, like ourselves, is also in direct contact with the corporeal.

World Soul and the physical universe

Plotinus' explanation for the way in which Soul produces and controls what is below it is an extension of the idea of double activity: Soul's essential, and therefore internal, activity necessarily produces an outer activity in its image; the contemplative activity of Soul, therefore, produces a lower level of contemplative activity as an image of its cause. This idea can be employed to explain individual souls as images of a higher soul activity, and, in turn, their own activity within the universe, as well as to explain the World Soul and its further activity in the physical universe. Sometimes Plotinus seems almost to envisage a series of image levels, the final one of which, termed 'nature', at its lowest level of activity, can no longer exercise the power of contemplative reflection on its prior but simply produce. This is the final expression of Soul's power and the weakest level of contemplation. The concept of a living power which animates the physical world in some way is found in the earliest Greek philosophers and is clearly expressed by Plato in the *Timaeus* and later by the Stoics.[4] Plotinus is also indebted to Aristotle's notion of 'Nature' which he interprets as the immanent power of the World Soul. Like Aristotle's nature *physis* does not deliberate,[5] but it is nevertheless for Plotinus a cognitive or contemplative power:

> If anyone wants to attribute to it understanding or perception, it will not be the understanding or perception we speak of in other beings; it will be like comparing the consciousness of someone fast asleep to the consciousness of someone awake. Nature is at rest in contemplation of the vision of itself, a vision which comes to it from its abiding

> in and with itself and being itself a vision; and its contemplation is silent but somewhat blurred.[6]

In some ways this unconscious rational power is the analogue of the contemplative activity of Intellect which lies 'above' discursive reason. For at the level of Intellect, too, there is no conscious awareness in the sense of self-awareness, since the Intellect would then consist of two elements, thinker and thought. But, of course, in other respects the two levels are quite different; for example, the contemplation of Intellect is in no sense blurred. Nevertheless even the lowest activities of soul are in some way 'thoughts':

> For the other lives are thoughts in a way, but one is a growth-thought, one a sense-thought. How then are they thoughts? Because they are rational principles (*logoi*). And every life is a thought, but one dimmer than another.[7]

This dim 'cognitive' activity does, however, have something in common with the higher activity of the World Soul which also excludes deliberation, which remains the special characteristic of human reasoning. For human reasoning, when it deals with things of this world, is deliberative. It plans its moves. The reasoning of the World Soul is for Plotinus above this; its reasoning is not one which calculates but is one where its object is more at one with itself. Nature, too, though on a lower level, does not calculate. Plotinus expresses this in a vivid way by personifying 'nature' and putting words into its mouth. He compares its activity to that of geometers in producing diagrams.

> And my act of contemplation makes what it contemplates, as the geometers draw their figures while they contemplate. But I do not draw, but as I contemplate, the lines which bound bodies come to be as if they fell from my contemplation.[8]

This reminds us of the Pythagorean and Platonic notion of the production of everything from number and the production of lines from points, geometrical figures from lines and solids from geometrical figures – in a word the production of a physical universe from the incorporeal and ultimately from the One.

But as well as this decreasing power of contemplation and of the *logos* which it transmits, matter is also seen as a partner in the creation of a world that is less perfect than its archetype. For the physical body, too, on which soul impresses form, is partly responsible for the comparative weakness and plurality of the final product insofar as it is unable to accept in full the form given to it.[9]

The presence of Soul to body

Soul is present to body in two ways. In the first place soul moulds matter so that it acquires a bodily form. Second, soul comes to that body to make it into a living and perceiving body.[10] We will postpone the difficult question of where matter came from in the first place.[11] Yet whether the issue is the presence of soul to matter or to body, the mode of this interface between the corporeal and incorporeal is for Plotinus one of the most difficult and serious of all questions. He has a number of approaches to the solution of this problem. We will begin with the negative arguments, which exclude inadequate explanations, before discussing his positive theories.

It is frequently and emphatically denied that the soul is in any way present in a spatial sense. It is not contained by the body. Rather the reverse is the case and the body is in soul like a net in the sea:

> It is as if a net immersed in the waters was alive, but unable to make its own that in which it is. The sea is already spread out and the net spreads with it, as far as it can.[12]

Nor is soul in the body as though in a substrate,[13] since in this case it would not be separable. Plotinus is probably thinking here of Aristotle who regarded the soul as a kind of immanent form which could have no separate existence after the substrate, the body, ceased to exist. Aristotle denied the existence of Platonic Forms as independent substances but had no problem, of course, with the notion of immanent Form so long as this is not seen as a substance, i.e. an entity which can exist of itself. Plotinus manages this issue by distinguishing clearly different levels of Form and, in particular, recognising the importance of immanent Form.[14] In fact for Plotinus there are more than two levels of Form, transcendent and immanent. Form for him is present at every level of reality beginning with Intellect, which contains the forms, or archetypes of everything, as intellects. It becomes progressively more pluralised at each successive level. (The term often used by Plotinus for form at each successive level is *logos*, an expression or manifestation which is sometimes seen as continuous rather than consisting of discrete stages, and thus constituting a progressive diminution of power.[15]) Thus immanent form is seen as the final manifestation, or effect, of a power. In this way he can make use of Aristotle's immanent form as an expression of the lower soul's powers in the body, while retaining the independent reality of soul itself.

Nor is it present like a part in a whole. He is probably thinking here of the Stoics, for whom the soul, or mind, was conceived of as a spark or part of the divine fire. But such a theory, however attenuated the notion of fire, is in the end a physical theory that involves spatial criteria.

On the positive side Plotinus explores three ideas to help explain the relationship of the corporeal to the incorporeal, the analogy of light, the concept of transmission of power and, last, the active power of perception.

Analogy of light

The presence of soul to body is compared to the way light or fire is present to air. Light, Plotinus claims, is not mixed with the air as though it were a physical entity placed side by side with portions of air, and yet it is present to the whole. In fact it is the air which is in the light for the air moves while light stays still.[16] Here Plotinus upholds the notion that the body is within the soul. Elsewhere he models the light analogy to fit the more traditional way of talking about the soul in the body.[17] He asks us to envisage a luminous mass around which is a transparent sphere so that the light shines throughout the sphere. We are now invited to dematerialise the luminous body by removing the bulk but leaving the light. It is not now possible to say that the light is in any one place or comes from any one place. It is equally distributed over the whole sphere. The analogy is strengthened by a further factor; for Plotinus light is incorporeal. The body at the centre of the sphere is luminous not in itself but because it is illuminated by light which transcends it:

> For it is not in that it is body that it has the light, but in that it is luminous body, by another power which is not bodily.

This thought experiment can also be applied to the sun: the light of the sun is everywhere, but if light is incorporeal the sun as a body is responsible only for mediating it. It is because the sun is a body that we appear to be able to point to a spatial source for the light.

But since the light is an immaterial self-subsisting substance, i.e. not dependent on body for its existence, we may think away the body of the sun and think only of the power of light. The result would then be that

> The light would not have begun from there [where the sun was] and you would not be able to say whence it came, but it would be everywhere as one and the same; it would have no beginning and no starting-point anywhere.

Elsewhere[18] Plotinus argues that light is an activity independent of a substrate. In doing this he takes a strong line against the Stoics who regarded light as material and Aristotle who saw it as a modification of the air. It is, he argues, an activity just as independent of a bodily substrate as is the life and activity which we call soul. And like any incorporeal power it takes its origin in the intelligible world, in fact from the One as the Good. This is an obvious reference to Plato[19] who compares the Good with the light which illuminates and makes intelligible the objects of thought.[20] For Plotinus 'light' is not a metaphor but a strong analogy: that is an analogy which not only provides an instance at another level of reality of what is to be explained, but an instance at the same ontological level. For, like intelligible power, the power of light functions at all levels as it unfolds from the One down to its function in illuminating physical objects. It is then not surprising that Plotinus is one of the main sources for the special role of light in subsequent metaphysics.

Transmission of power

After his list of rejected explanations for the relationship of body and soul in IV.3, Plotinus shows himself more receptive to the idea that the soul is present in the body as a steersman in a ship.[21] This at least accounts for separation, for the steersman may live independently of the ship, but it still relies on spatial concepts since he is present on only part of the ship. Even if we claim that the steersman is present in the rudder (and by extension to the ship as a whole) by means of his skill, there is still the spatial distinction between the steersman and the tool that he employs (the rudder) and to which his skill is transmitted. This is, however, an analogy that might be refined if, for example, we look at the relationship of soul to body in a physiological context. Plotinus accepts the notion advocated by certain physicians[22] that the brain is the centre of the nervous system and both receives and transmits with respect to the senses. This theory accounts for the plurality of senses and also their unity. But, Plotinus argues, the actual 'power' of the senses is not to be located spatially in the brain or anywhere else in the body (for it is omnipresent) but in the soul which is linked to, but not located in, the brain. The brain is simply the point where soul power is first manifested or actualised in the body, whereas the soul, the 'workman' or equivalent of the steersman, is the source of the 'power' itself:

> But it would be better to say that the beginning of the actualisation of the potency [of perception] is there. For it was necessary that at the point from which the organ (tool) was going to be moved that the power of the workman, as we may call it, which was appropriate to the tool should be fixed; or rather not the power – the power is everywhere – but the beginning of its actualisation at the point where the organ begins.[23]

In VI.4 he exploits a similar analogy but in a different way.[24]

> For, from what has been said, it is not correct to divide that same up into the many, but rather to bring back the divided many to the one, and that one has not come to these many, but these because they are scattered have given us the impression that also that has been taken apart, as if one were to divide what controls and holds together into parts equal to what is controlled. And yet a hand might control a whole body and a piece of wood many cubits long, or something else, and what controls extends to the whole, but is not all the same divided into parts equal to what is controlled in the hand; the bounds of the power, it appears, extend as far as the grip, but all the same the hand is limited in extent by its own quantity, not by that of the body it lifts and controls. And if you were to add another length to the body which is controlled and the hand was able to bear it, the power would control that too without being divided into as many parts as the body has.[25]

A hand holding a long piece of wood, insofar as it can support the wood, may be seen as controlling it rather as the soul controls the body. The power, however, is a property of the hand and, though physically bound by the confines of the hand, is not actually divided around the hand. Now if you were to add to the length of the wood and the hand were able to continue supporting it, the control of the hand would be spatially extended in the wood, but the hand would remain the same. Thus the area affected may be divided into parts while the controlling hand remains undivided. Plotinus now asks us to abstract the corporeal bulk from our notion of the hand:

> Well then, what if someone supposed the corporeal bulk of the hand to be taken away, but left the same power which also before held up what was formerly in the hand? Would not the same power, being without parts, be present in the same way in it all, in every part?

The idea of controlling power has a rich background, and Plotinus may have had in mind Aristotle's *de anima* [26] when in VI.4.7,8f he founds the non-spatial relationship of being to the physical world on the power of being to 'control and hold things together'. Aristotle's argument is, however, somewhat different: if the soul holds together and gives unity to the body, it cannot itself be a corresponding plurality because there would then be need of a further principle to provide its unity, and we would then call this the soul. Since this would lead to an infinite regress we must hold that soul is unified. The essence is, however, similar: that which unifies (holds others together) can do so only if it is not itself characterised by the diversity which it holds together.

Another way of exploring the idea of soul's power is linked with the theory of double activity which we have mentioned above.[27] The soul's powers that are immanent in body are seen as an image of the essential activity of soul. And so the man of this world is the activity of the soul and not its being.[28] The perception which is active in the body is an image of perception at the transcendent level. Thus the activity in the lower man is an image of the activity/being of the higher. The lower soul is a *logos* of the higher which is in turn a *logos* of intellect.[29]

This notion of power is one of Plotinus' most successful approaches to the difficult question of the presence of Form to matter. Plato himself had found a difficulty in explaining their relationship. In the apparent self-criticism of the *Parmenides* Plato seems finally to have conceded the difficulty when he clearly rejects the analogy of the presence of one Form to many instances expressed in terms of a sail covering many sailors, since each sailor is in fact covered by one particular part of the sail.[30] And if this is so the transcendent Form appears to be divided into parts. Then there is Plato's recourse to the notion of 'participation' which is famously criticised by Aristotle as a misleading metaphor.[31] Both Plato and Aristotle seem, in different ways, to have been unable to extricate themselves altogether from the notion of a spatial element in their attempts to explore the relationship of incorporeals and corporeals, although one might argue that the notion of participation was an attempt by Plato to avoid spatial concepts and the (admittedly colourful) language of the *Timaeus* is intended to suggest the same. As for Aristotle, even when he posits an obviously incorporeal reality (the first mover) he is still tempted to express its relationship to the world in terms of the spatial:

> Moreover the movement must occupy either the centre or the circumference, since these are the first principles from which a sphere is derived. But the things nearest the movement are those whose motion is quickest.[32]

When dealing with the presence of incorporeal powers Plotinus is no doubt responding to both Plato and Aristotle, though in a broader sense he is simply dealing with a fundamental metaphysical problem, which had been articulated by Plato and Aristotle, but which presents itself in subsequent philosophical debate. It is striking, for example, how often Plotinus sets out to show that there is such a thing as incorporeal reality and to explore its nature. He finds it necessary to battle incessantly against purely materialist notions, represented primarily by the Epicureans whom he likened to heavy birds which can scarcely take off from the ground.[33] Incorporeal substance, however self-evident a part of the mental furniture of a Platonist, needs constant clarification. And that is inextricably bound up for Plotinus with the relationship of the incorporeal to the corporeal, a problem to which he dedicated an individual treatise. *Enneads* VI 4 and 5, originally one treatise which was later divided by Porphyry, are devoted to *The presence of Being, one and the same, everywhere as a whole*. Here we have no mention of the three great levels of incorporeal reality, the One, Intellect and Soul, but the enquiry is pursued by condensing them into one generic term, Being, and thus concentrating on the essential question of the nature of the incorporeal and the mode of its presence or connection with the physical. In it Plotinus proceeds in two ways: by analogies, examples of which we have seen; and by the articulation of a metaphysical statement of the nature of Being's presence. The latter emerges as the apparently paradoxical statement that Being is everywhere and nowhere. This key statement which at once removes the notion of spatial relationship (nowhere) and affirms the causal expression of relationship in terms of power (everywhere) became a standard Neoplatonic concept.

Of these two main ways of dealing with the relationship of corporeal to incorporeal reality the power concept, with the analogy of the piece of wood moved by a hand, is probably the easier and more convincing for us. The power of the hand is felt as effect and thus present in the piece of wood as a whole, though it is nowhere spatially present. Plotinus proceeds to dematerialise the analogy by asking us to imagine the corporeal bulk of the hand to be removed, leaving only the power. For him an actual example of such manifested power may be seen in light considered as something incorporeal and thus separable from its apparent physical source, the sun. This instance is, of course, not one we can accept unless we believe light to be incorporeal, although as an analogy it has explanatory power and, by dematerialising light, Plotinus could defuse the trouble Plato found himself in with his light analogy in the *Parmenides.*

Perception as an active power

Plotinus stresses the active rather than passive nature of soul's relationship to body. In sense-perception, for example, he argues strongly against Stoic theories which stress the soul's passive reception of impressions like seal stamps on wax. Plotinus, on the other hand, argues strongly for the active participation of the soul. This activity of the soul may be seen not only at the point of contact with the physical object, but also in the inner working of the soul. For the soul's contact with the external object is achieved not simply by incoming stimuli but by an outgoing and therefore active power of the soul which goes to meet them. Similarly in the inner working of the soul the central perceptive powers are able to distinguish different sources of impressions, i.e. hearing, vision, touch, only by the fact that they actively process the impressions and that, too, not as physical imprints but as incorporeal and 'intelligible' items. What are seen and heard

> Are not by nature impressions or affections, but activities concerned with that which approaches [the soul].[34]

But we tend to think that perception consists in being struck by an object which then somehow makes an impression on our souls. The point is then made even more clearly in the case of hearing when the sound is seen as impressed and therefore carried on the air, like letters written on the air which the soul can then read when they are brought near to us. The active power of the soul is here expressed in the idea of 'reading' the sounds. Even with taste and smell where the physical contact of body and external object is more apparent Plotinus is clear that the soul is active even though there are bodily affections; for all perceptions of such things

> are acts of knowledge of the affections distinct from the affections themselves.[35]

The individual soul

Soul, like Intellect, is both one and many, the many including the World Soul which relates to our souls as a kind of elder sister. This relationship of one to many is sometimes described by Plotinus as a one and many, as opposed to Intellect which is a one-many, an indication of the less unified plurality of Soul. It is also described in terms of genus and species and Plotinus goes on to apply the double activity theory to the individual souls themselves, whose inner activity is thinking and whose external activity reaches out to the physical world.

> And the activities of these (individual souls) are double: that which is directed above is intellect, that which is directed below is the other powers in proportion and order; the last of them is already grasping and shaping matter.[36]

This plurality of souls is not caused by embodiment, but is of the very nature of soul itself and exists before embodiment.[37]

The divided mission of the soul

How can we reconcile the descent of the soul to give life to the body with the injunction to separate ourselves from the body? The more negative view of the soul's descent into the world is expressed by the notion of the soul's self-assertion (*tolma*). This self-will is identified with a kind of self-indulgence on the part of the soul which leads it further and further away from its intelligible home.[38] It is more closely identified with a meddlesomeness in what does not concern it and a desire to do its own thing rather than retain its link with what is above it.[39] This tension between the urge of soul to immerse itself in body and its natural affinity with the transcendent is addressed directly in Plotinus' treatise on *The descent of the soul into bodies.*[40] This is the treatise which commences with the striking 'autobiographical' experience of the transition from transcendent contemplation to awareness of the bodily state.

> Often I have woken up out of the body to my self and have entered into myself, going out from all other things; I have seen a beauty wonderfully great and felt assurance that then most of all I belonged to the better part; I have actually lived the best life and come to identity with the divine; and set firm in it I have come to that supreme actuality, setting myself above all else in the realm of Intellect. Then after that rest in the divine, when I have come down from Intellect to discursive reasoning, I am puzzled how I ever came down, and how my soul has come to be in the body when it is what it has shown itself to be by itself, even when it is in the body.[41]

Plotinus then goes on to state clearly the apparent paradox found in Plato himself that the function of the soul is to give life to the body when we are also told by him to separate ourselves from the body. The positive is found by Plotinus primarily in the *Timaeus* in which

> When speaking about this all he praises the universe and calls it a blessed god, and says that the soul was given by the goodness of the Craftsman, so that this all might be intelligent.[42]

The negative side is found in the *Phaedo, Republic* (the cave), and the *Phaedrus.* The descent of the individual soul to complete the universe is elsewhere described by Plotinus as an inner urge or law reflecting and putting into action the universal law by which soul gives life to body and expresses the pattern of the universe.[43] But the basic ambiguity and tension within Platonism is still maintained:

> The souls go neither willingly nor because they are sent, nor is the voluntary element in their going like deliberate choice, but like a natural spontaneous jumping or a passionate natural desire of sexual union or as some men are moved unreasoningly to noble deeds.[44]

In the end these two functions of the soul are partially reconciled by pointing out that what we must separate ourselves from is an over-immersion in the physical. The World Soul which also has contact with the physical world does not need to pay attention to the details of its charge. But it has only a general care of the universe, while we are set over a particular body. And yet the individual soul is individual not because of body, but even before embodiment, and our coming down to individual bodies is also an expression of the Intelligible model of the universe since we fulfil its every detail. The real danger is in a prolonged and over-involved association with body. We should try to curb the amount of attention we pay to the details of everyday life and attempt to imitate the way in which the World Soul controls the universe without becoming over-involved in it. This double mission is, then, reconciled in the case of the World Soul, which is able to relate to this world while remaining undisturbed in contemplation of its prior. In fact it not only performs the shaping and administrative functions within the physical universe but is also aware of this world.

> The Soul of the All has not become engaged in the worse kind of work and, having no experience of evils, considers what lies below it contemplatively and remains attached to the realities before it for ever; both are certainly possible; it can receive from There and at the same time distribute here.[45]

It is in this context that Plotinus also claims that even the individual soul can reconcile the life of contemplation with its bodily functions, since like the World Soul it too has a higher part which transcends this world. It is also significant that in discussing whether star souls have memory, a problem very similar to that of the World Soul's relationship to the physical world, he draws on parallels from human behaviour. He notes, for example, how, when we have grasped the totality of a task, there is no need to dwell on the details, or how in constant repetition of a task we are no longer aware of the individual movements;[46] we might cite the case of a musician who is not aware of his finger movements when playing his instrument. These ideas are accounted for by the fact that a sensation does not always penetrate further into the soul so as to become a perception; and a perception occurs only when the reasoning power is conscious of a sensation. One should also note in this account the stress on the active engagement of the soul which enables it to choose not to perceive irrelevant details.[47] All of these observations help us to understand how the individual soul can, like the World Soul, rule its body without being intimately attached to every detail of the process. On numerous other occasions Plotinus exhorts us to imitate the World Soul.[48]

Time and eternity

We have already had occasion to point out how Plotinus often seeks to correct our erroneous notion of process in our understanding of the intelligible world. Strictly the intelligible is not ordered in a chronological, but in a logical and causal, sequence. We, however, apply to it our own experience of order which is coloured by our experience of time. But the context for the Intelligibles is eternity. Hence the importance of examining our understanding of time and eternity. As so often, the determining parameters for understanding basic concepts are drawn from Plato, in this case his description of time 'as the moving image of eternity'. The importance of the two concepts for Plotinus is that they corroborate the distinction between the physical world of change and the stable world of the Intelligibles, and the dependence of the former on the latter. But they also serve to distinguish Soul from Intellect, since the outcome of the discussion also points to a distinction between what is in time, the physical world, and time itself which, it is concluded, is the life of the soul. The major discussion of time and eternity in the treatise dedicated to the topic[49] also demonstrates some important aspects of Plotinus' philosophical method, not least his engagement with the thought of his predecessors. The views of Aristotle, the Stoics and the Epicureans on time are all discussed. In the end he finds them wanting because they concentrate on the external manifestations of time rather than on what time is in itself. It is this concentration on what time is in itself, or what causes things to be in time, that leads him to give time a more elevated role than had his predecessors, as the life of the soul.

But the final delineation of time as soul life is only reached by a consideration of the nature of eternity. Eternity is not strictly to be identified with Intellect; for we say Intellect is eternal[50] and the predicate cannot be identical with the subject of predication. But eternity may be said to be 'in' or 'present to' (*para*) Intellect and their relationship to each other is not exactly reciprocal, since Intellect includes everything as a whole includes its parts, whereas eternity includes the whole all 'at once'.[51] Eternity, then, is more like an aspect of Intellect.

> The nature of eternity is contemplated in the Intelligible nature existing in it as originated from it, because we see all the other things, too, which we say are There existing in it, and say that they all come from its substance and are with its substance.[52]

Eternity is characterised neither by future, past nor present. We must be particularly careful to avoid regarding it as a kind of continuous present, a tendency encouraged by the application of the word 'always' to the concept of eternity in an attempt to make it more intelligible to our time-bound processes of conceptualisation. It is worth citing Plotinus' own words as a good example of the care he takes with the presentation of concepts, and in this case the beginning of a long history in the clarification of an important idea.

> But when we use the word 'always', meaning that there is not a moment when it (Being) exists and another when it does not exist, we must be thought to be expressing it in this way for our own sake; for 'always' is perhaps not being used in its strict sense, but, taken as explaining the incorruptible, might mislead the soul into imagining an expansion of something becoming more, and again of something which is never going to fail. It would perhaps have been better only to use the word 'existing'.[53]

But the importance of the concept of eternity does not end here, for not only does it help to illuminate the way in which Intellect timelessly thinks and produces, but it can also be applied to the life of the individual. For if 'well-being', the traditional goal of the philosophical life, is located at the level of intellect and thus of eternity, then the old question as to whether well-being increases with time can be side-stepped:

> Well-being must not be counted by time but by eternity; and this is neither more nor less nor of any extension, but is a 'this here', unextended and timeless.[54]

The good man enjoys the life of the true self, the level of intellect and true Being, outside time, just as his higher self remains unaffected when the lower self feels the pain of being roasted alive in the bull of Phalaris.[55] When we follow the causal sequence from Intellect and eternity to Soul and time we find the familiar transition from stability and unity to movement and plurality. And just as soul constitutes itself as an image of its prior and then produces the physical world as an image of itself, so too soul in the context of time constitutes its own life as an image of eternity and in turn creates as an image of itself the physical world in time. Time exists then on two levels – as the life of the soul and as the time perceived in the physical world where things are 'in time':

> Soul moving with a motion which is not that which exists There, but like it, and intending to be an image of it, first of all temporalised itself, making this instead of eternity, and then handed over that which came into being as a slave to time, by making the whole of it exist in time and encompassing all its ways with time.[56]

The striking neologism, a single verb, which I have attempted to translate by the word 'temporalised' indicates Plotinus' care to avoid any suggestion that soul is 'in time'. Of course we can say that soul operates in time through its lower powers, but the essence of soul is a life of reasoning that is characterised by succession, but not temporal succession, for thinking in a chronological sequence is a mark of the sort of discursive reason that deals with things in the physical world. For the disembodied soul (or the higher soul) the 'before' and 'after' involved in reasoning signify order (*taxis*) rather than time, just as in a plant the order begins from the root and extends to the top; for the observer who sees the whole plant at once this is an order of ranking rather than of time.[57]

Matter

We have spoken earlier of the presence of soul to matter. But what is matter, and is it created by something else or is it something independent? The earliest Greek philosophers had attempted to find some basic substance which would serve as the originating substance of the universe and its continuing base, something which could explain the coherence of the universe behind its changing face. Plato was more concerned to explore the nature of the form imposed on things than the basic substance on which the forms rested, although in the *Timaeus* he left some enigmatic suggestions for later Platonists to interpret.[58] Aristotle was more interested in elucidating the nature of what receives form, and bequeathed a doctrine of 'matter' as bearer of immanent form which was to be exploited by Platonists. In a simple sense the basic material out of which something is made could be considered to be its matter, e.g. the bronze which is given form to become a statue. But even the bronze has qualities of its own: it has colour, weight, dimensions. Strip away all qualities and we are left with what Aristotle called 'prime matter'. This Plotinus identified with the 'receptacle of becoming' in Plato's *Timaeus*[59] which for Plotinus was not to be identified with space, for space implies a qualification of some sort. Matter has no qualities whatsoever, it is non-being, but not absolute non-being. It is non-being in the sense of possessing no form whatsoever – it is not any thing. But if it simply did not exist it could not be the recipient of form. It has, therefore, a kind of quasi or bastard existence.[60] Matter is not merely the absence of form, it is also the contrary of substance and of form,[61] a status which again invests it with a kind of existence and leads Plotinus to identify it as absolute evil. Matter is also identified with privation, a reversal of Aristotle's distinction of matter (substrate), privation and form.[62] Whereas for Aristotle privation is replaced by form, Plotinus rejects the idea that the substrate changes at all. Thus matter always remains what it is, utter privation, and any change is simply that of forms playing over its surface like clothing placed on a body.[63] In another passage the matter of the universe is described as an adorned corpse, something which has no life or qualities of its own.[64]

Plotinus sometimes suggests that deficiency of form is partly, at least, caused by the intractability of matter in receiving it. This almost endows matter with an active quality and the image used to describe this aspect of matter, that of a distorting mirror, does nothing to dispel this. But the intention is not to endow it with a completely independent and active existence of its own as may be seen from its being compared to the darkness around the edges of a light beam. This analogy suggests a causal efficacy which is vested in the very diminution of the light: but the resultant effect has no positively active existence, for darkness is simply the absence of light. It is, perhaps, the nearest Plotinus comes to Proclus' more precise and clear categorisation of matter as a *parupostasis*, a by-product with no existence of its own:

> That huge illumination of the supreme pouring outwards comes at last to the extreme bourne of its light and dwindles to darkness; this darkness, now lying there beneath, the Soul sees and by seeing brings to shape.[65]

The inability of matter to affect form is strongly argued elsewhere by Plotinus.[66] The same applies to soul as we will see.

Another important point is that like Proclus, later, Plotinus wished to avoid the notion of an independent matter which could provide the opposite pole to the One and so create a completely dualist system. And so Plotinus firmly rejected the notion of matter as a second principle, a sort of counterpart of the One. For he sometimes seems to identify the One as the creator of matter, and sometimes the soul.[67] In the case of the latter it appears to be the lowest phase of the World Soul which is responsible for creating something which is 'indefinite'. This is in some way parallel to the production of intelligible matter as the indefinite outpouring from the One. But there the similarities cease, as if Plotinus is at pains to distance soul from the production of what he has designated as evil. In the production of matter the soul does not look to its prior in contemplation but to itself and produces something that is 'totally different from itself' and 'absolutely indefinite'. And whereas intelligible matter turns back upon the One to receive form from it, physical matter has no such power, but is enformed by soul which takes the initiative and turns back again towards it:

> But when it looks at the image [matter] again, as it were directing its attention to it a second time, it forms it and goes into it rejoicing.[68]

Just as matter acts as a substrate for form in the physical world, so too in the intelligible world there is an exact analogue: an intelligible matter which acts as a kind of substrate to form. It is hardly likely that Plotinus would have conceived of such an idea had it not been already embedded in tradition. The idea of the imposition of limit, represented by unity, on the indefinite, represented as two-ness or the dyad, can be traced back to Plato, both more generally in the *Philebus* and explicitly in his so-called oral teaching.[69] Plato probably took the idea from Pythagoreanism and it found its way back into a Platonised Neopythagoreanism which formed one of the many strands leading to Neoplatonism. The concept was particularly exploited by Plotinus to explain the generation of Intellect from the One. The outpouring of power (the external power) from the One is at first indefinite and represents the stage of procession. This power then reverts on the One to be enformed and limited by it, thus representing the stage of return. The enforming or limiting of the indefinite is in some respects parallel to the enforming of matter. But there are important differences. Intelligible matter is not evil, it is an outpouring and expression of the One and has a positive power.

Evil

Since we have introduced the notion of evil, a few words of further explanation are required. If the ultimate cause is the Good and thus the source of all that is good in the world, what, it may be asked, is the source of evil? Plotinus wished to avoid the dualist answer that there is a parallel principle which acts as the source of evil, since in his view this would leave us with two primary principles whose relationship would either be one of chance or depend on a yet higher principle, which would lead us back to monism.[70] Monism, as we have just seen, is the course that Plotinus took in identifying matter as evil and in deriving matter from Soul and, since Soul is derived from the One, matter is derived ultimately from the One. Evil may be regarded under two heads. There is natural evil by which we mean the disorders of nature which cause destruction, such as earthquakes, tidal waves, droughts, and there is moral evil which is usually ascribed to the responsibility of individual moral agents. Plotinus' attitude to the first of these is to subsume any irregularities as being subplots in a universally good pattern. It is often not possible for the nearby observer to see the overall pattern and to understand how what might seem to him to be a present disaster might in fact be working to some overall good. This idea, which reflects Stoic arguments for universal providence, came naturally to a Platonist for whom the Intelligible world represented the overall pattern of the universe derived from the Good, which is then expressed in physical reality through the limiting categories of space and time. Imperfection and failure there is in the world and it has to be explained. Plato himself, though unambiguous about moral responsibility and the goodness of god, had nevertheless provided an opportunity for speculation with his reference to disorderly motion in the *Timaeus*. Some Platonists had interpreted these ideas in an almost dualist way.[71] Plotinus avoided this and resisted even more strongly those contemporary elements, including Gnostics within his own school, who taught that the physical universe was in itself evil and the product of an evil creator.[72] But how does evil and disorder come into the world? For Plotinus it is not the ordered universe which is evil but its underlying substrate, matter: that which, though itself without extension or bulk, is the means by which the incorporeal is in the end expressed in terms of bulk, the final manifestation of the incorporeal in the limiting spatio/temporal context of corporeality. As the ultimate bearer of the last vestiges of form it thus has a causal role in facilitating the creation of body, which is matter enformed. Evil, as disorder and imperfection, is thus not left unexplained. Yet while fundamentally opposed to good and form, as we explained above, it is also ultimately derived from them.

When we turn to the individual the situation is complicated by the factor of individual responsibility. But in the case of the individual soul, too, matter plays an important role as a cause of evil. At root we have the same basic issue as in natural evil. The final physical expression of the soul's power in producing and giving life to a body is a natural function of its own nature as soul, but embodiment is at the same time clearly identifiable as a possible diversion of the soul's inclinations. It is in this sense that matter, in presenting an occasion for moral evil, may be said to be evil for the individual soul. But in saying that matter is evil Plotinus is not claiming that matter of itself is the sole cause of evil nor that the individual soul is completely innocent of moral faults. Matter is evil insofar as it is the contrary of form which is good. But, as we have already seen, form is not affected by matter and neither is soul. For soul too is impassible and can never become intrinsically evil, since if it became intrinsically evil it would, like matter, have no qualities or form. But in this case it would cease to be soul. The soul can, however, become evil incidentally. Now, Plotinus thinks that this can happen only when the soul comes into contact with matter. But though matter may be a necessary cause of evil in the soul, it is not a sufficient cause. For this, the contact with matter must be combined with a tendency in soul to greater involvement with matter than is necessary. Since the individual soul may avoid this over-involvement it may be held responsible for moral failure. This is clearly expressed in Plotinus' treatise on providence when he makes the distinction between natural disorders and moral evil.[73]

We have in this chapter strayed between universal and individual much more than in our chapter on Intellect. This was inevitable given the much closer identification of the centre of the human individual with the level of Soul. But just as in the case of Intellect the ultimate unity of Intellect with individual intellect plays an important role in understanding human destiny, so also the highest potential of the human soul is best understood in the comparison with the World Soul as an expression of universal Soul. It is to this reintegration of the individual with the universal at every level that we must now turn.

5

THE RETURN OF THE SOUL

We began our introduction to the philosophy of Plotinus by concentrating on the individual as he finds himself in this world. For the individual, as thinker and speculator, is the starting point of Plotinus' philosophy. The fate of the individual, his descent into body and return to the Intelligible world, form the core of his thinking. Throughout the *Enneads* we are strongly conscious of his direct appeal to his listeners (and readers) to look to their own experience and apply his teaching to the way in which they conduct their lives. Many of the treatises are structured to appeal in this way. For example V.1 begins with an invocation to us as individuals to realise the situation we are in and to recognise the different levels of reality which make up our Being, from discursive reason to intellect. These then point to the macrocosm to which we are related at every level. Having established the existence and nature of the three Hypostases from an examination of our own nature, Plotinus then adverts to their gradual unfolding in the history of philosophy whose culminating point is, of course, Plato. The treatise closes by returning to these levels of reality within ourselves:

> Now just as these three exist for the system of Nature, so, we must hold, they exist for ourselves.

And he concludes with an appeal to us to turn our attention to what is above:

> Hoping to hear a desired voice we let all others pass and are alert for the coming at last of that most welcome of sounds: so here, we must let the hearings of sense go by, save for sheer necessity, and keep the soul's perception bright and quick to the sounds from above.[1]

This practical concern is the main motive of Plotinus' metaphysical speculations and, although in the end the ultimate goal is the mystical flight of the 'alone to the alone', even that high pinnacle is not, as we shall see, an entirely self-centred goal.

Ethics

Although Plotinus was as firm as any philosopher of antiquity that the good life is also the virtuous life we will not find in the collection of Plotinus' treatises any great direct concern with the details of ethics. There is a treatise on the virtues (I.2), but even here the realm of practical ethics is dealt with in a fairly summary way as a stage on the way to the higher contemplative virtues. This treatise set a sort of standard pattern for a schema of levels of virtue which was formalised by Porphyry and further elaborated by later Neoplatonists. Plotinus himself did not intend to establish a fixed scale of virtues but rather to explore the way in which the traditional cardinal virtues – wisdom, justice, courage and self-control (sophrosyne) – could be expressed at the different levels of man's moral and spiritual activity. And this is the main point: for Plotinus the level of everyday living, which represents the field for the exercise of moral virtue, is only one level at which the human individual is active. It is, therefore, necessary to establish how the traditional invocation 'to live virtuously' might be applied to the other, more important, levels of activity. More particularly how is it conducive to the primary aim advocated by Plato in the *Theaetetus*[2] that we should flee this world and become like god? To become godlike became the primary aim for Platonists and in Plotinus it is identified as the return of the individual to his original godlike state at the level of intellect:

> For he himself is the god who came thence, and his own real nature, if he becomes what he was when he came, is there.[3]

What we would more normally associate with virtue and ethical discourse is, then, for Plotinus only the base level for the ascent of the individual to the higher aspects of his nature. It is represented by the so-called political virtues, virtuous activity as it is exercised within the community in everyday affairs. The following levels are all concerned with the separation of the soul from this world and thus are above the level of ethics as it is normally understood. Plotinus here finds a place for Plato's concept of virtues as purifications[4] which help to initiate the soul's turning away and rejection of this world; next comes the more positively inclined stage of reasoning where there is the first recognition of the higher realm, and last the so-called intellectual virtues representing our activity at the level of intellect. Plotinus' distinction between the state of being purified and the resultant state of having achieved purification was later formalised into two distinct levels of virtue. This is not exactly what Plotinus meant but the two states do present important differences of emphasis that he elsewhere carefully notes with his usual sensitive psychological observation based on the practical experience of how we can turn our attention to transcendent values, as for example in V.1:

> A double discipline must be applied if human beings in this pass are to be reclaimed, and brought back to their origins, lifted once more towards the supreme and One and First. There is the method, which we amply exhibit elsewhere, declaring the dishonour of the objects which the soul holds here in honour; the second teaches or recalls to the soul its race and worth.[5]

The fact that Plotinus does not dwell on the details of 'political virtue' does not mean that they are irrelevant. In fact they represent a prerequisite for the ascent of the soul, but are, to a large extent, taken for granted by him and, therefore, do not, in his view, merit detailed discussion. Moreover we will see that when the good man rises to the higher levels of virtue, these will in their turn also provide guidance for the conduct of life at the level of political virtue, an idea strikingly expressed in the analogy of the effect of a wise man on his neighbour:

> Just as a man living next door to a sage would profit by the sage's neighbourhood, either by becoming like him or by regarding him with such respect as not to dare to do anything of which the good man would not approve. So there will be no conflict: the presence of reason will be enough; the worse part will so respect it that even this worse part will be upset if there is any movement at all, because it did not keep quiet in the presence of its master, and will rebuke its own weakness.[6]

His own life and the way in which he looked after orphans and cared for the well-being of his companions are adequate testimony that Plotinus was not indifferent to the problems of everyday living. We may also note that ethical theory does not figure prominently in the writings of other Neoplatonists and yet there is increasing evidence that Neoplatonists were concerned with the activities of practical living. We can point, for example, to the 'ethical' interpretations of certain Platonic dialogues in the later set reading curriculum or the commentary of Simplicius on the *Encheiridion* of Epictetus, the practical and even political involvement of Porphyry, Iamblichus and Proclus,[7] and not least the evidence from Arabic philosophers, who had an interest in ethical theory, of Neoplatonic commentaries on Aristotle's ethical writings.[8]

At the end of the treatise on virtue Plotinus affirms that the man who possess the higher virtues must have the lower virtues at least potentially; but does he actually practise them? This is a difficult question since in the case of some virtues the higher level is characterised by a quantitative difference, e.g. moderation of passions at one level and total suppression at a higher level. His conclusion is cautious and relative: perhaps the possessor of the virtues will know exactly what they can provide for him in different circumstances. That is, although the individual may now be living a different life, that of the gods, this higher level will still impinge in some way on his worldly activities. To see exactly how we must look elsewhere.

Contemplation as a universal and individual activity

We have already seen how Plotinus extends what he sees as man's own core nature as a thinking or contemplative being to the whole of the macrocosm whose very existence is maintained by a hierarchy of contemplative realities. It is within this context that he gives us a further suggestion as to how to reconcile external action with the inner contemplative ideal. When Plotinus describes the lowest manifestation of Soul power as the weakest form of contemplation, producing an object (the physical world) which no longer has contemplative power, he compares this activity to that of individual humans. The man who has weak powers of contemplation tends towards being purely a man of action. Because he cannot internalise his thoughts, he projects them outwards in the form of an external object or act. Even this is an instance of the importance of vision because he does this precisely so that others and he himself may see the object. The wise-man, however, has no need *for himself* of any external object; he can internalise his contemplation. But, and this is of prime importance, the internal contemplation of the wise-man still produces some external object or result, virtuous action. In his case it is the natural expression of his internal activity, just as Intellect or Soul through their internal power produce an external manifestation:

> Everywhere we shall find that making and action are either a weakening or a consequence of contemplation; a weakening, if the doer or maker had nothing in view beyond the thing done, a consequence if he had another prior object of contemplation better than what he made. For who, if he is able to contemplate what is truly real, will deliberately go after its image?[9]

The external virtuous act will then accompany the internal disposition of the virtuous man; in fact it is its natural consequence. Virtuous activity will flow from the wise-man, but its successful manifestation is not essential for his well-being. It may be the case that material circumstances hinder the completion of the external act. For example it is not always possible to put into actual practice a heroic decision or to express one's generosity if all one's possessions are taken away. But, we may ask, is the wise-man not to notice that he is practising practical virtue? And if so the external act seems quite irrelevant and, perhaps, bereft of personal value. There are two things to say about this. First we should pay attention to Plotinus' general attitude to the physical world and to virtuous action as exemplified in the many comments he makes about the beauty of the world and his many expressions of sympathy and understanding of the human condition. The physical world and action within it does have value (after all, the world is divine!); it is only in relation to its superior and cause, when its value is relativised, that it falls into second place. Second, and more technically, we should note that he can explain and justify the possibility, and even necessity, of our being aware of, and involved in, our external actions. The awareness is, however, qualified: we should not be so aware of, and involved in, these external actions that we are 'dragged down' into them and away from the very principles that are their source. If we also take into account Plotinus' understanding of different levels of consciousness[10] we will find that he holds a coherent theory of how contemplation can be reconciled with action. For the theory allows for our full awareness of our worldly predicament while, at the same time, our higher self is active at a different level of consciousness. Such a theory provides the necessary metaphysical support for an ethics of transcendence, where we can be fully alive at both the empirical and intellectual levels simultaneously, just the point that Porphyry makes about Plotinus in the *Life*: 'he was present both to himself and others at the same time'.[11] In fact such a person lives at the higher level in eternity. His lower, time-bound life, will be automatically informed and perfected by this higher life and will, at the same time, be a life which can be lived in full awareness of its surroundings and of the ethical demands they make.

The mysticism of intellect

We have already seen in an earlier chapter[12] the immense gulf separating the state of reasoning, which might rightly be said to constitute the essential nature of the soul, and that of intellect, which for Plotinus represents a transcending by the individual of his human status, but not, we should emphasise, of his status as an individual, since for Plotinus each of us has been and can again become a god. Indeed the ultimate nature of the individual is his godlike status, some trace of which he retains even in his embodied state. And this godlike status is the state of intellect. On several occasions when Plotinus is referring either to the individual intellect or to what, in the end, is the same, the universal Intellect, he can speak in terms reminiscent of those used by him to describe the union with the One. Although Plotinus goes to every conceivable length to make coherent his concept of intuitive intellect, in which subject and object are identical and yet separate, he appears to be struggling to express something almost as difficult to comprehend discursively as the union with the One itself. When we add to this the dimension of eternity we find ourselves in even greater conceptual difficulties. And it is precisely at the level of intellect that we find the conjunction of the higher self in eternity and the empirical discursive self within time. This intersection of time and eternity within the individual is important for Plotinus' philosophy of human activity within the world. It may be useful to draw a parallel with the Buddhist distinction of two levels of mystical experience, one a continuous encounter that informs our daily lives and the second an intermittent experience of greater intensity at a higher level.[13] The same distinction is found in some Christian mystics.[14]

Plotinus was very positive about our capacity to rise to the level of Intellect by our own efforts and without the sort of divine help which both Christians and the later Neoplatonists thought was necessary. One important indicator of this optimism is his statement that part of our soul has not descended but always remains in the intelligible realm. He is clearly aware that this idea is something of a departure from received Platonism.

> And if one ought to dare to express one's own view more clearly, contradicting the opinion of others, even our soul does not altogether come down, but there is always something of it in the intelligible.[15]

This view was also shared by Porphyry and Theodorus of Asine, but vigorously rejected by Iamblichus and Proclus.[16] Probably the main reason why Plotinus held it was to provide some kind of secure link between the individual intellect and soul.

Removal of all and apophasis as experience

The practical counterpart of *apophasis* or negative theology is the removal from oneself of all that is alien, *aphairesis.* It is the One as the Good which is the ultimate source of our desire to strip away the alien from ourselves in our return to the One which is totally itself and without any otherness.

> For all things reach out to that and long for it by necessity of nature, as if divining by instinct that they cannot exist without it.[17]

This removal of the alien begins with the soul realising that in embodiment it has not only attached itself to a physical body but has also acquired a sort of shadow self in the external power of the soul which gives life to the body. We must disassociate ourselves as much as possible from this alien self.

> So we must ascend again to the good, which every soul desires. Anyone who has seen it knows what I mean when I say that it is beautiful. It is desired as good, and the desire

> for it is directed to good, and the attainment of it is for those who go up to the higher world and are converted and strip off what we put on in our descent.[18]

Plotinus compares it to chipping away at a statue until it is made beautiful, an idea which might have been suggested by Plato's memorable comparison of the embodied soul to the seagod Glaucus, who is covered in encrustations which must be removed before we see the true original soul.[19] Having removed the alien from ourselves and finally come near to the One, we must now continue to strip away everything from our vision of it. We must allow nothing to be added to it.

> When you have put away all things and left only himself, do not try to find what you can add, but perhaps there is something you have not yet taken away from him in your mind.[20]

Mystical union with the One

We have already seen that the practice of negative theology or apophasis is, for Plotinus, not simply an intellectual process of abstraction, but one of personal moral and spiritual preparation. The logical end of the metaphysical dynamic of procession and return is, for the individual, the return to, and union with, the ultimate cause, the One. But this is a spiritual as well as conceptual imperative and it is this aspect that is described by Plotinus in terms which we call a mystical experience. In its broadest definition mysticism may be described as a close contact with the divine or some other power in a timeless experience. There have been many attempts to categorise different types of mysticism. Although it is worth mentioning these different varieties of mysticism we will find that Plotinus does not readily fall into any one category and this may well be true for most mystics. Three main categories have been suggested: monistic, pantheistic and theistic. In a sense Plotinus falls into all three. He would certainly maintain that the final union with the One is an experience of unity with the one, single ultimate principle of everything; but his experience is equally of union with the divine. And while he does not describe an experience of unity with the natural world and Neoplatonism does not identify the universe with god as the ultimate principle (although the universe is divine), in another sense the One as cause of everything may be said to 'contain' everything, and so the experience of unity with it may be seen as an experience of unity with everything. We may also point to his description of our soul as an 'intelligible universe' since our intellect is one with the universal Intellect which embraces all the intelligible archetypes:

> For the soul is many things, and all things, both the things above and the things below down to the limits of all life, and we are each one of us an intelligible universe.[21]

These categories, then, are perhaps more useful in showing the richness of Plotinus' mysticism than in delineating it. All of them are attempts to describe objectively what is always a subjective experience. Plotinus himself gives adequate warnings in this regard, when he refuses to describe the experience itself. Indeed it is not possible to describe it. We can only point to it and point others to it, so that they can make the journey themselves.

> The soul runs over all truths and all the same shuns the truths we know if someone tries to express them in words and discursive thought; for discursive thought, in order to express anything in words has to consider one thing after another; this is the method of description; but how can one describe the absolutely simple? But it is enough if the intellect comes into contact with it; but when it has done so, while the contact lasts, it is absolutely impossible, nor has it time to speak.[22]

Since the soul is now in eternity it does not have 'time' to speak. To speak signifies here the sequential thought of discursive reason, whether manifest 'in time' or characterised by the time-life of soul. The mystical experience takes place in the context of eternity which transcends time. Plotinus makes a clear distinction between what Plato calls the 'study' of the One and our actual experience of it. The former can be conducted through discursive reason but, if it is to lead to experience, we must employ other means:

> We are put on the way to it by purifications and virtues and adornings and by gaining footholds in the intelligible and settling ourselves firmly there and feasting on its contents.[23]

When we look to the ways in which the mystical ascent is made we can stand on more objective ground as observers. I would like to point to three different ways of preparation, though they need not be mutually exclusive. Each of them involves mental effort of some kind. There is first the way that stresses physical preparation – relaxing the body, taking account of the physical environment, its sounds and texture. Second there is the way that stresses traditional prayer and contemplation of scriptural or religiously expressed ideas. And last there is the way that relies primarily on the contemplation of philosophical concepts. While Plotinus' approach falls, no doubt, largely within the last mode, there are indications that he is at least aware of the value of the other modes, even if they were not prominent in his practice. For example before approaching the difficult problem of how Intellect thinks he asks his listeners to 'invoke god himself, not in spoken words, but stretching ourselves out with our soul into prayer to him, able in this way to pray alone to him alone' [24] and he continues the religious theme by invoking the analogy of an inner and outer sanctuary. In the outer sanctuary are the statues and images of the divinity that lies within, the one accessible to reason, the reality accessible only to intellect. Earlier in the same treatise, in exhorting us to envisage the entry of the World Soul into the physical world, he uses language reminiscent of the preparation for a contemplative exercise:

> Let not merely the enveloping body be at peace, body's turmoil stilled, but all that lies around, earth at peace, and sea at peace, and air and the very heavens.[25]

Even if such adjuncts to contemplation were of little importance to Plotinus, it is, however, appropriate at this stage to note their value to mystical ascent as they are found in later mysticism, both Eastern and Western, since this may be helpful in understanding that the more ritual and religious tendencies of later Neoplatonists need not exclude genuine mystical experience.

Although we must prepare ourselves for the final union with the One, and Plotinus lays great stress on the fact that it is within our own power to attain it, in the end it is necessary to be patient. You cannot force yourself upon it, for it comes on its own terms and its appearance, like the sun over the horizon, is often sudden. This idea is not only traditional,[26] but probably reflects actual experience and metaphysically preserves the independence of the ultimate principle. In fact the One is not simply a passive object of desire, but exercises a causal attraction over us which is parallel to the causal efficacy with which it secures our existence.

> Every one of those beings exists for itself but becomes an object of desire by the colour cast upon it from the Good, source of those graces and of the love they evoke. The soul taking that outflow from the divine is stirred; seized with a Bacchic passion, goaded by these goads, it becomes Love … its very nature bears it upwards, lifted by the giver of that love ... there is some glow of the light of the Good and this illumination awakens and lifts the soul.[27]

The One is here described as a 'giver' and what it gives as an 'outflow' from itself, in some way analogous, we might suppose, to the outflow which is constitutive of Intellect. The later Neoplatonists made much more of this active power of the One in proportion to their diminishing of the soul's own power to raise itself. It is important to note that the basis of the idea exists already in Plotinus, but equally important to realise the difference in emphasis and in consequent practice. Plotinus does not recommend the use of special methods, whether spiritual or ritual, by which this outflow from the One can be channelled.

The final contact with the divine is a personal experience, but there is also a sense in which we are not cut off from others. In the analogy of the circle which is often used by Plotinus to describe our relationship with the One it is important to note that others are involved:

> And there must also be in us the principle and cause and god of Intellect. He is not divided, but abides, and as he does not abide in place he is contemplated in many beings, in each and every one of those capable of receiving him as another self, just as the centre of a circle exists by itself, but every one of the radii in the circle has its point in the centre and the lines bring their individuality to it. For it is with something of this sort in ourselves that we are in contact with god and are with him and depend upon him; and those of us who converge towards him are firmly established in him.[28]

This passage refers both to our normal relationship of dependence on the One for our very existence and, for example in the final phrase, to our special relationship in mystical return and union with him. It is important to note that there are many radii which meet at the centre, which is therefore a communal point, as much as the single point of the lone mystic. In another version of the circle analogy the individual is a particular circle and the One is the central point at which the centres of all the individual concentric circles coincide.[29] Again we have the stress on the plurality of points or individuals at the single centre. The 'individuality' which is brought to the centre reinforces the notion and also alerts us to the fact that for Plotinus the individual is not annihilated in the mystical union. Just as Plotinus is concerned to maintain a certain difference between thinker and its object in Intellect, while at the same time arguing strongly for their identity, so too, when it comes to union with the One, he tries, however paradoxical it may seem, to retain the individual somehow even in the midst of total union. As we approach the One we feel that we are entering into nothingness, as though we are making a leap into the dark and fear to fall over the precipice. But even the union itself, since it is a step beyond Being, is also, in a sense, a step into non-being and nothingness. Here at last we are divested of all self-absorption:

> He was one himself then, with no distinction in him either in relation to himself or anything else; for there was no movement in him, he had no motion, no desire for anything else when he made the ascent, no reason or thought; his own self was not there for him, if we should say even this.[30]

But he is still concerned with the 'self'. We should note the caution in that last phrase; Plotinus is not here saying that the individual is obliterated but only that he is no longer aware of his own individuality; and yet he hesitates finally to admit even this. A little later in the same passage we have further reference to the 'self' now in complete conformity with the One, but still present:

> When it (the soul) goes down it comes to evil and so to non-existence, but not to absolute non-existence; and when it travels the opposite way it comes not to something else but to itself; and so when it is not in anything else it is in nothing but itself. But when it is in itself alone and not in Being, it is in that [the One]; for one becomes oneself not Being but beyond Being by that intercourse. So if one sees that one's self has become this, one has it as a likeness of the

> divine; and if one goes on from it, as image to original, one reaches the end of one's journey.

We have stressed throughout our discourse on Plotinus the importance of that central problem of Greek metaphysics, the reconciliation of unity and plurality. Even at the height of man's achievement, his final union with the Unity absolute, the individual is not abandoned. The final words of the treatise leave us in no doubt; for an encounter, for unification, there must be two. Man's final goal is a 'flight of the alone to the alone'.

Part II

THE DIFFUSION OF NEOPLATONISM

6

PHILOSOPHY AND RELIGION

In his *Life of Plotinus* Porphyry records how Amelius, the senior student of his circle, once invited Plotinus to accompany him on a pious visitation of the local temples.[1] Porphyry and his companions were baffled by Plotinus' response: 'They ought to come to me, not I to them.' Of course Plotinus was not denying the existence or importance of the gods but rather placing a priority on the inner spiritual life and a philosophical rather than ritual encounter with the divine. Porphyry, too, would have understood that Plotinus was not denigrating the gods, but as a man of his age would have found it difficult to understand how a philosophical veneration of the divine could be totally separated from what we might regard as the externals of worship. In a similar way Plotinus accepted the efficacy of magical spells but chose not to ascribe any great importance to them. Magic, according to Plotinus, was simply a way of manipulating or appearing to manipulate the sympathy which existed naturally between all objects in the physical universe; for the artificial use of these links may not in fact indicate any result other than what would have naturally occurred.[2] And although these patterns in the universe are ultimately reflections of the intelligible cosmos,[3] Plotinus does not exploit this transcendent cause as Iamblichus was later to do. And as a further indication of the neutral value he places on magic he regards the moral state of the petitioner in a magical ceremony as irrelevant.[4] The picture is similar when we turn to prophesy, an integral part of traditional Greek religious experience. It too is a product of universal sympathy and thus operative only within the material world. The sharp division between the immaterial realm of Intellect and the lower world is illustrated by his comment that diviners used *logismos* rather than intellect.[5] Nor does he deny that events may be foretold by using the stars, but this is achieved only by learning the various combinations of signs in a way similar to that in which we can draw conclusions about a person's character and actions by examining his eyes. For stars are members of the universal order as we are.[6] But in his view man could transcend the sublunary world to a transcendent world where the links of sympathy, on which magic depended, had no power. In this attitude he stood somewhat outside the common view of his fellow philosophers who mostly accepted the necessity of coming to terms in some way with these factors and of integrating them more explicitly into their world view. It is thus not surprising that other Neoplatonists engaged more profoundly with issues presented by magic and traditional religious practice. It is difficult to say to what extent, if at all, this interest was influenced by the advances made by organised Christianity. More likely than not it may be ascribed, in its initial phases at least, to the tendency of philosophers, and especially Platonists, to accept conventional expressions of piety. But what is surprising is the new intensity of this acceptance which was linked with a desire to find explanations for religious phenomena and to integrate all religion in a coherent way into a philosophical structure. It would be quite wrong to regard this tendency as a relapse from Plotinian rationalism into superstition. Rather it represents one of the first profound attempts to relate philosophy to religion.

Porphyry, who was one of the first to manifest this interest, came from a mixed Semitic and Greek background in Tyre. He had studied in Alexandria before joining the official Platonic Academy in Athens. He was as much a philologist and polymath as a philosopher. No doubt his own background combined with his general interests was at least partly responsible for his interest in the religious aspirations and expressions of different cultures. Whether he had once been a Christian is uncertain and is probably due to an element of black propaganda raised against him by subsequent Christian writers anxious to dispel the effects of his attack on Christianity published in his book *Against the Christians.* For one so interested in religion and sympathetic to Judaism it may seem surprising that Porphyry undertook this attack. But one has to realise that Christianity's exclusiveness was bitterly resented by many pagan thinkers for whom religious inclusivity and syncretism came second only to an intense loyalty to local pagan cults which embodied their notion of society and belonging. These are both aspects of pagan religion which were deeply appreciated by Porphyry. There were, of course, serious metaphysical and doctrinal grounds for his rejection of Christianity. For example the idea of the supreme god, as opposed to a minor god or daimon, descending to earth was unthinkable for a Neoplatonist. But in fact the larger part of his attack was occupied with a devastating scholarly attack on the veracity of the *Book of Daniel* which at the time was regarded by Christians as an important prophecy of the present triumph of the Church and thus confirmation of the authenticity of its mission. Porphyry's proof that the 'prophecy' was in fact composed after the events was a serious embarrassment for this claim.

One cannot overestimate the enthusiasm for learning and enlightenment that brought Porphyry first to Athens and then to Plotinus in Rome. He was clearly deeply influenced by Plotinus' originality although resistant at first to many of his ideas. In religious matters, however, he had a quite different temperament from Plotinus. And although he shared some of the views of Plotinus on the efficacy of magic, he also displayed a more traditional affinity to religious practice. He interested himself not only in the minutiae of symbolic interpretations of ritual objects such as statues of divinities, as we can see from the fragments of a work *On Statues*,[7] but with the role of religion in the way of return to the highest principle, what he could call the 'salvation of the soul'. He was concerned that the way offered by philosophy seemed in reality open to a limited number of people. No doubt he believed, like Plotinus, that it is possible for everyone to turn to philosophical contemplation, but, unlike Plotinus, he saw that realistically this was not very likely. In fact the majority of men found some kind of spiritual consolation in religion. His work *On the Philosophy from Oracles* seems to be aimed at just such an audience who required the support of religious sanction for their philosophical beliefs.[8] Moreover certain mystery religions even proclaimed their power to unite their adherents to god in a relationship that had more in common with the Platonic assimilation to the divine than that fostered by traditional religious practice. One particular ritual of salvation, developed from a text called the *Chaldaean Oracles* which had been composed in the second century AD by a certain Julian the 'theurgist' and his son, became especially important for Platonists, partly perhaps because the teaching of the 'Oracles' themselves was already deeply influenced by Platonic ideas. The word 'theurgy' itself suggests divine intervention in the world[9] mediated by a priest or theurgist and the Oracles' ritual of salvation, which was intended to raise the soul to union with god, looked very similar to what Plotinus and Porphyry would term 'magic' in its mode of operation. It seems, however, that these 'Oracles' attracted Porphyry's attention as he wrote an extensive commentary on them. This interest was part of Porphyry's wider concern to discover a 'universal way of salvation' by which he probably meant one that was open to all types of men and to all nations.[10] Evidently he did not find it, primarily because he could not bring himself to accept that the god of religion was the same as the god of philosophy. Religious rites could raise one only to a certain limited level – to the gods of the heavens, i.e. the gods who are within the physical universe. To reach a higher level required moral rather than just ritual purity, and also intellectual effort. He rejected the idea that the higher soul could be affected by ritual means. According to Augustine he distinguished two aspects or levels of the soul, one called the 'spiritual soul' (*anima spiritalis*) and the other the 'intellectual soul' (*anima intellectualis*). The latter dealt with Forms and is clearly the equivalent of the higher soul in Plotinus while the former, which alone is susceptible to 'magic' and ritual, is the equivalent of the lower soul in Plotinus. Its name also suggests that it is closely connected with the semi-corporeal soul vehicle or *pneuma* which would also serve as an enabling link to the powers of universal sympathy used by magic.[11] He also expressed concern that certain kinds of ritual, which might be termed magic, could be employed to do harm to an individual by his enemies,[12] while in general much ritual was concerned with mundane requests rather than salvation.[13]

None of this, however, prevented him from affirming the necessity to perform the traditional rituals of civic religion. He is happy to recommend the worship of traditional gods and to admit in general terms the efficacy of religious rites. While objecting to animal sacrifices in accordance with good Pythagorean practice, he can state as a view he evidently agrees with that one of the aims of sacrifice is to seek benefits.

> There are moreover, three reasons altogether for sacrificing to the gods: to honour them, to give thanks, or from the need of good things. As [we behave] to good men, so too we think we ought to offer the gods first-fruits. We honour the gods because we want evil to be averted from us and goods to be provided for us, or because we have had benefits from them, or simply to honour their condition of goodness.[14]

Elsewhere he expresses the seriousness of the sacrificial intent; offerings to the gods are not made 'casually but with full commitment'.[15] And for him intent and moral probity are essential if religious ritual is to have any value. Like Plato[16] he links traditional piety with the security and well-being of the city-state. Even animal sacrifice, though very much a second best to the sacrificial use of plants and fruits, may still be performed even by philosophers.[17] Porphyry has a problem with animal sacrifice, but more importantly seeds of doubt had also been sown in his mind about the status of traditional piety in general. For the philosopher sacrifice and traditional prayer are not really necessary. Both in *On Abstinence*[18] and in *Philosophy from Oracles* he extols the practice of spiritual prayer and sacrifice:

> For God, as being the father of all, has indeed no lack of anything; but it is well for us when we adore him by means of justice, chastity, and other virtues, making our life itself a prayer to him by imitating him and seeking to know him. For seeking to know him purifies us, while imitation of him deifies us by bringing our disposition in line with his.[19]

When it comes to the intimacy of personal advice, for example to his wife Marcella, a delicate balance may be observed. In this context he is not concerned with the issue of abstinence from eating meat but with the more basic opposition of the philosophical and the ordinary life, the contrast between the intellectual prayer of the philosopher and the verbal or ritually enacted prayer of traditional religion. The former is, in his eyes, clearly higher in value. Indeed ritual and prayer without virtue is useless and a good man can honour and become godlike through virtue alone, which means that the highest level is reached only through virtue.[20] But this does not rule out traditional piety entirely. And so Porphyry can go on to encourage his wife in its practice – 'the greatest fruit of piety is to honour the divine in the traditional way'.[21] And in a well-phrased understatement he neither affirms nor denies the benefits of reverencing the altars of the gods which 'when honoured do no harm, and when neglected bring no benefit'.[22] But in the end it is the internal disposition, intention, purity and clarity about the real nature of the divine that are the determining factors. As a chain of citations demonstrates,[23] it is a traditional piety modified by Pythagorean strictures, but it is active, ritual piety nonetheless.

Porphyry's position is in general very much like that of Plato. He accepts the necessity for traditional civic (and private) religious rites and, in a vague way, he also accepts their efficacy as something more than social convention. Like Plato[24] he denies that the gods can be compelled in any way. Moreover religious rites are particularly important for the state. But Porphyry goes further and expresses the beginnings of a doubt. Nevertheless when he continues to uphold traditional religion this is not a sign of his insincerity. He is not simply trying to avoid social or legal sanctions; nor does he accept religious practice as simply socially or psychologically useful, but like Plato thinks it is in some way objectively effective. His problem is that his enquiring mind had been prompted by the new phenomenon of theurgy to pose serious questions about the way in which ritual can be efficacious. Theurgy was a philosophico-religious construct, taking both its means of expression and its goals from Platonism and from religion. For a philosopher like Porphyry who had a profound respect for religious systems it was not possible to ignore it. Theurgy appeared to offer the possibility of reaching the same goal as the philosopher by means of ritual. It therefore raised the question of divine causation in ritual in a more demanding and explicit way than traditional religion. It is then not surprising that Porphyry should have extended the enquiry about causality to all aspects of religion.

His greatest difficulty was to account for the way in which the gods can be said to intervene in our lives through rituals: what is the role of the priest? Does he have power over the gods or do they come of their own free will? How can what is lower (the priest) summon or even compel what is higher (god)? How do the different levels of gods relate to each other? How are the different types of divinity (gods, daimones etc.) differentiated? How do oracles work? What is the causal efficacy of ritual objects and words? These and many other questions were posed by him in a work purporting to be a letter to an Egyptian priest by the name of Anebo. It is important to grasp that this work, known as the *Letter to Anebo,* was not an attack on pagan religion or ritual, but rather a series of questions and problems. Indeed in some cases Porphyry provides possible solutions. For example, in the case of prophecy, three alternative explanations are offered: that it is caused by a god drawn down through an invocation, or that the prophecies are produced by the soul itself, or finally that prophecies are doubly caused and come from our own soul and from external divine intervention.[25] Although Porphyry finds some purely magical activity distasteful, it is clear that he accepts the genuineness of most religious phenomena. What concerns him is the search for an explanation of them and a resolution, if possible, of some of the philosophical problems they raise. There is nothing disparaging, for example, about his careful description of the experience at the main oracular sites of Delphi, Didyma and Claros.[26] Porphyry is not disputing the fact of prophecy but enquiring as to the 'way in which prophecy is sent to men from the gods'.[27] Even when dealing with the rites of the theurgists about which he had serious doubts, he at no point accuses them of deliberate deception but finds an explanation in the powers of the soul which, he claims, the theurgists are too ready to trace back to transcendent divine powers. In other words he accepts their power but limits it, as Plotinus had done, to the physical world. But however innocent Porphyry's intentions were, his enquiries and tentative answers left a vulnerable impression of the nature of pagan religion.

The *Letter to Anebo* survives only in fragmentary form and is, for the most part, to be reconstructed from citations in a reply written by Iamblichus, a work which is traditionally called *On the Mysteries (de mysteriis)*, in which he was concerned to correct Porphyry's dangerously inconclusive enquiry. This work, which is admittedly rather long-winded at times, has undeservedly been castigated as a charter for irrationalism. In fact Iamblichus can sometimes be quite critical of the use of ritual; for example, when it is employed for nefarious ends.[28] His primary concern is to counter what he regards as the dangerously ambiguous position which Porphyry had adopted, but in doing so he creates what could be termed the first systematic philosophy of religion. Porphyry, he claims, had asked the wrong kind of questions in the wrong kind of way. Philosophy, religious ritual, and theology, each demand a different mode of discourse. All three are expressible in words and to that extent open to reason, but the ways in which reason is applied are different in each case. Porphyry, he argues, had illicitly confused these modes of discourse, in particular by presenting the issues involved in ritual in terms of philosophical categories; this presents serious distortions when we attempt to explain the causal factors involved in a ritual act where we have god, theurgist, and a material element, whether sacrificial or verbal.

> I think I must say something about these things in a more theurgical manner ... It is not thought that connects the theurgist with the gods ... Rather the efficacy of the ineffable acts, which operate divinely beyond all thought, and the power of the symbols, which are understood by the gods, effect theurgic union. This is why we do not set these acts in train by thinking: for if this were the case their

> activity would be intellectual and determined by us; but neither of these is true; for, without our thinking, the symbols themselves and of themselves effect their own operation; and the ineffable power of the gods, to whom they refer, itself and of itself recognises its own images.[29]

Here Iamblichus is trying to stress the causal efficacy of the divine which is above human thought, and thus obviating the objection that the priest or theurgist could be said to influence or even manipulate the divine. Yet at the same time he finds a role for the ritual act or object. In fact these transcend the human agent who simply employs them. Then do these ritual acts and objects affect the gods in any way? Such an idea is mitigated in two ways: first by locating the efficacy of the acts not in the material object itself but rather in its power as symbol, and second by stressing the independence of the gods who are not directly affected by this power but rather *actively* recognise and therefore respond to it – 'the ineffable power of the gods, to whom they (the symbols) refer *itself* and *of itself* recognises its own images'. This is a brave attempt to maintain the independence of the gods while at the same time not diminishing the power of the ritual act. It might be legitimate to draw an analogy with the philosophical concern in later Platonism to come to terms with the independence which subordinate principles display despite their dependence on their priors.

But let us return to the human element in religious ritual, for Iamblichus goes on to say that this too has a causal force, but as an accessory rather than a primary cause. In this way, he argues,

> The divine is itself aroused by itself without receiving into itself any starting point for its own activity through any of the things below it.

And so by invoking the distinction of primary and secondary causation, an idea which can be traced back through the Stoics to Aristotle and Plato,[30] he seeks to remove a misunderstanding, that the gods are forced by men. It is remarkable that this theurgic discourse is rational to the extent of employing causal ideas of a philosophical nature. But this does not contradict his claim to be using the correct form of discourse, since what he has presented us with is not a philosophical analysis, whose veracity rests solely on the application of rational principles and argument, but the select application of an appropriate philosophical principle to a case whose complete understanding lies beyond the powers of human reasoning. We should employ reason and rational argument while being aware of their limitations. What may present a contradiction in the physical world may be reconciled at a higher level. There is in fact a transcendent logic to govern relations among transcendent realities.[31] One of its most important characteristics is the way in which it operates by analogy, for in this way demonstrative arguments and discursive concepts can be used to 'indicate' the nature of the higher level, i.e. to predicate without maintaining every implication of the predicates. And Iamblichus frequently emphasises the inadequacy of philosophical discourse for theological and ritual subjects by moving to a form of discourse that employs a different vocabulary. We must also remember that Iamblichus is not attempting to give an *explanation* of ritual phenomena, for explanations belong to the realm of philosophy, but rather simply to defuse apparent contradictions.[32] This cautious and economical approach to the application of rational explanations to religious phenomena can already be seen in Plutarch who expresses the idea that we must do our best to give explanations of religious phenomena, while recognising that they are in the end beyond our full comprehension and that the human mind has its own limitations.[33]

Whatever the weaknesses of this nascent sacramental theology it represents an advance on Porphyry's well-meaning probings. Although the role of theurgy never ceased to be an issue among Neoplatonists, Iamblichus' work laid the foundation on which later philosophers such as Proclus could elaborate a rich texture of pagan ritual and myth as a parallel expression of their philosophical views and practice. It would seem that later Neoplatonists laid differing stress on the importance of theurgic ritual. A later commentator can categorise them as either philosophers or hierophants, the former including Plotinus and Porphyry, the latter Iamblichus and Proclus.[34] The emperor Julian was himself initiated by Maximus, an extreme adherent of Iamblichus. But it should be pointed out that there were other more moderate thinkers such as Aedesius who was severely critical of Maximus.[35] Julian clearly had deep religious inclinations. His devotion to the god Helios is full of Neoplatonic concepts which he probably owed ultimately to Iamblichus.[36] The god Helios is worshipped both as the physical sun and as an intellectual god. He is the product of the One, identified with Plato's Idea of the Good, and is made manifest at the intellectual level. His goodness is bestowed on the intellectual and the intelligible gods, a division initiated by Iamblichus and based on an attempt to define more clearly the thinker and the object of thought in Plotinus' Intellect. Throughout his exposition of this solar theology the influence of the sun analogy in Plato's *Republic* is evident. In particular the concept of incorporeal light and its effusion from the One plays an important role. In memorable words he expresses some of the fundamental tenets of Neoplatonism, the beauty of the universe, its eternity, its dependence on the intelligible world and ultimately on the transcendent One, which, as in Plotinus, is the 'centre' of all things:

> This divine and wholly beautiful universe, from the highest vault of heaven to the lowest limit of the earth, is held together by the continuous providence of the god, has existed from eternity ungenerated, is imperishable for all time to come, and is guarded immediately by nothing else than the fifth substance whose culmination is the beams of the sun; and in the second and higher degree, so to speak, by the intelligible world; but in a still loftier sense it is guarded by the King of the universe, who is the centre of all things that exist.[37]

The One is the cause of beauty, perfection, unity and power. Something of Julian's own spirituality is seen in this very personal description of his experience:

> But this at least I am permitted to say without sacrilege, that from my childhood an extraordinary longing for the rays of the god penetrated deep into my soul; and from my earliest years my mind was so completely swayed by the light that illumines the heavens that not only did I desire to gaze intently at the sun, but whenever I walked abroad in the night season, when the firmament was clear and cloudless, I abandoned all else without exception and gave myself up to the beauties of the heavens; nor did I understand what anyone might say to me, nor heed what I was doing myself.[38]

Proclus, too, was a convinced practitioner of theurgy, wrote hymns, and considered the Chaldaean Oracles, on which he wrote an extensive commentary, to be on a par with Plato's *Parmenides*. His rather austere daily routine, which included lectures and then private seminars with his research students, began and ended with ritual prayers.

But to what extent did theurgy extend into the experience of Intellect and of the One? And if it did extend to these levels how far was it accompanied by external, ritual elements? We recall that Porphyry (and of course Plotinus) had rejected the efficacy of theurgy outside the bounds of the physical universe which was subject to the laws of sympathy. But both Iamblichus and Proclus admitted its efficacy to the higher realms, though both of them seem to have made a distinction between a higher and lower range of theurgic activity, the latter restricted to the physical needs of life and the former embracing spiritual benefits which included the attainment of intellectual unity and union with the One itself. It is unlikely that either Iamblichus or Proclus thought that such heights could be reached without living a moral and philosophical life, but their attraction to theurgy was dictated both by their own religious proclivities and by loyalty to the ideal of Hellenic traditional religion as well as by important metaphysical considerations. Even Plotinus had noted that when we are united in intellect and with Intellect we are no longer living a human life.[39] Of course he goes on to embrace this superhuman aspect of the individual within a broad concept of the individual as embracing both human and divine dimensions – 'We are each of us an intelligible universe.'[40] This is too imprecise for Iamblichus and Proclus, both of whom locate the individual clearly at the human level of discursive reason. Our intellect is only an illumination or *ellampsis* of intellect proper. Thus attaining the level of intellection was not simply a matter of engaging a higher aspect of ourselves, but of transcending ourselves, something which required the operation of external forces of some kind. Plotinus had himself briefly intimated that we are aided to union with the One by some kind of overflowing power from the One, but external assistance becomes a prerequisite to ascent both to Intellect and to the One in Iamblichus and Proclus, and, more importantly, is channelled through rituals. If we add to this the doctrine of Henads,[41] a means of expressing metaphysically the omnipresent power of the One, we see that Proclus had at his disposal a metaphysical concept which could be used to explain how certain herbs and stones, the material of ritual, could somehow express a special relationship with the One. In fact, in a further observation, Proclus noted that the higher a power the further its effects were felt.[42] Thus the highest of all, the One, was causally effective throughout the system to the very lowest entities, which

Intellect and even Soul had not reached. Such a concept naturally provided added reason for accepting the special power of the sort of simple substances used in religious rites. We must, however, remember that for Proclus it was not a stone in itself that could achieve these special effects but rather the power invoked by the symbolic links with the One. Moreover it is doubtful whether Proclus thought that the highest stages of union were achieved in a purely mechanical ritualistic manner, though the utility of ritual was at least theoretically upheld. At the end of a short fragment entitled *On the Hieratic Art*[43] he tells us that to ascend to the higher levels we must abandon 'nature and natural activities' and employ 'primary and divine powers', implying that we should move from the use of corporeally immanent symbols or henads to those present at higher metaphysical levels. In a fragment of a treatise *On the Chaldaean Philosophy* we read the following:

> Our hymn to the father is not one composed of words, nor the preparation of ritual actions. For since he alone is imperishable, he does not accept a perishable hymn. Then let us not hope to persuade him by a novel downpour of phrases or by a display of skilfully contrived actions. God loves uncontrived beauty. Then let us raise to god as a hymn our own efforts to become like him.[44]

Although the idea expressed here is something of a commonplace, it is still a very striking indication of the more spiritual side of theurgy as understood by Proclus. This comes out even more in Proclus' discussions of the unknowability of the One in which at times something very close to a Plotinian expression of the mystical experience of the One can be found. Another interesting pointer to Proclus' understanding of the final experience of the highest levels of reality is found in his analysis of stages of ascent. He speaks frequently of 'the flower of intellect', a faculty of the individual at the very highest level of discursive reason, by which he can be in contact with the Intellect. But to be in contact with the One some yet loftier power is needed. However, instead of whittling away the individual to some higher point Proclus declares that the One is grasped by the 'flower of the whole soul', going back as it were to a lower but more comprehensive level of our being. And he adds his reason – 'for we are not just intellect alone, but also reason, opinion, application and will'.[45] This attempt to reintegrate man at the highest level of his spiritual aspirations as a complex of mind, mental and moral effort may help us to understand how he could combine philosophy and religious sentiment.

We may conclude by mentioning the broader context in which this symbiosis of philosophy and religion was achieved. The Stoics had already led the way in demonstrating how the gods of traditional religion could be accommodated within an essentially monotheistic philosophical system by being regarded as aspects of the single divine substance. The task of creating a comprehensive Platonic theology was probably well under way by the time of Iamblichus. One of its manifestations may be found in Julian and in the work of Sallustius, probably one of his mentors.[46] But its fullest expression is found in Proclus and particularly in his massive *Platonic Theology* in which he attempted to integrate the divine systems of traditional Greek religion, Pythagoreanism, Orphism and the Chaldaean Oracles into one grand system based on a universal order derived from Plato's *Parmenides.* The details of the endless levels of divine beings – henadic, intelligible, intelligible and intellectual, intellectual, cosmic, etc. do not concern us. What is important is the attempt to embrace the whole of pagan Greek religious experience into a single system which could also take in the greatest works of Greek literature. For Homer was also a theologian.[47] However alien such an undertaking might seem to us, it nevertheless reflected an important factor in Greek attitudes, that their religious and cultural experiences were irretrievably interwoven, what Julian could call 'Hellenism'.

7

THE DEVELOPMENT OF NEOPLATONISM

While Plotinus is the foundation stone of Neoplatonic thinking and recognised as a key figure by Proclus, for example,[1] subsequent thinkers made many important contributions to the deeper understanding and even resolution of difficult issues. Porphyry, as the editor of Plotinus' treatises, may be regarded as his immediate successor although it is not known whether Porphyry continued the school of Plotinus or even had one of his own. Since his thought is so close to Plotinus we will consider him first before moving on to those later Neoplatonists whose thought is known to us to any considerable extent. It will be more convenient to deal with these together under the heading of particular problems. We know most about the thought of Proclus but must constantly bear in mind that many of the ideas which receive their clearest exposition in his thought may go back to his predecessor Syrianus and, in many cases, to Iamblichus whose works have survived in mostly fragmentary form.

PORPHYRY

It is worth dwelling for a moment on Porphyry since he is undoubtedly a key transitional figure in the history of Platonism. Apart from his religious views which we explored in the last chapter he does not seem from what survives of his writings to have made any really radical departure from the stance of Plotinus, although our picture is distorted by the fact that what survives of his voluminous output is largely ethical in character and his metaphysical writings are almost entirely lost. His original home was Tyre but he spent time in Alexandria, in Athens and finally in Rome where he joined Plotinus for some six years. He kept in contact with his homeland but it is difficult to say whether he ever lived there again for long periods or remained in Italy after the death of Plotinus in 270. He was largely responsible for the spread of Plotinus' ideas which he sent to his former teacher Longinus in Athens. He also edited and published Plotinus' treatises (we owe our edition to him) and wrote commentaries on them. These are now lost but they probably helped to explain and even popularise Plotinus' difficult ideas. In addition he is responsible for giving a more prominent place to Aristotle's works as a preliminary course of study to those going on to read Plato and to the fostering of a harmonisation of Plato and Aristotle that had been a project of earlier thinkers and was to be developed further by Iamblichus. Some of Porphyry's commentaries on Aristotle's logical works were still being used in universities in the eighteenth century. It is often thought that Porphyry's espousal of Aristotelian logic betrays a sharp difference between himself and Plotinus. But in fact Plotinus' own criticism of Aristotelian logic is not as severe as has been maintained, for its inadequacy as a logic for transcendent metaphysics does not preclude it from being admissible in the sublunary sphere.[2] Probably the aspect in which he most differed from Plotinus was that of religion as we have seen in the previous chapter.

It is, nevertheless, interesting to trace some of the major concerns which Porphyry also shared with Plotinus and to note some of the small ways in which he differs in emphasis or philosophical style from him. Like Plotinus he shows a deep concern with the way in which soul is present to body and the connected issue of the omnipresence of being. This is expressed in a number of ideas occuring in the *Sententiae,* a curious fragmentary survival which looks at first sight like a summary of Plotinian doctrines and may have served as an introduction to philosophy. Indeed he often seems to be citing or paraphrasing the *Enneads.* But the very tightness of the format – it is broken up into summary-like treatments of specific topics which are often over-compressed and formulaic in expression – leads to a rigidity and lack of flexibility in conveying what in Plotinus is more open and flexible. This is already a step towards the later attempt by Proclus to achieve greater intellectual clarity by precise hierarchical distinctions. Among the many Plotinian doctrines which are found in this work, we may begin by referring to the twofold activity concept which Porphyry expresses in terms of a secondary 'power' which is related to body. The notion of relation – *skesis* – becomes almost a mantra and is employed by him to avoid falling into language which suggests spatial contiguity. Soul is not present in its substance or hypostasis but by the projection of a power which can come into relationship with a body.

> Incorporeals are not present to bodies or mixed with them in their hypostasis and being, but give them a share in a certain power relative to bodies which is produced by an inclination towards them, for the inclination produced a second power relative to bodies.[3]

Thus the soul is active in the body by means of this secondary power but at the same time remains an independent entity. The soul's essential 'unity' with other souls is not lost on embodiment; it is the activities of soul which are hindered and apparently pluralised.[4] These 'activities' are another expression for the secondary power which unfolds into a multiplicity as it is deployed in the body. This unfolding is also characterised as a gradual diminution in power. In another work Porphyry engages with Stoic notions of 'mixture' in an attempt to account for the soul's presence in the body. The soul is not mixed in with the body as one material substance with another. And although there is a total interpenetration of soul and body, analogous to the Stoic notion of the interpenetration of bodies,[5] we must realise that the soul as an incorporeal substance cannot be spatially present to body. But this does not exclude its being 'related' to body. Rather we should say that body is in soul. Porphyry is not rejecting the idea that the immaterial can in some way be localised. He is not objecting to pointing to a definite 'somewhere' when we talk of soul, but to the way in which we say it is present 'here': we should say that 'it is active here', not 'it is here'. We should not confuse relational activity with being in place.

Another manifestation of this concern about the relationship of soul to body is Porphyry's interest in a quasi-material intermediary between body and soul which he terms the *pneuma.* This concept helps him to account for the continued existence of the lower powers of the soul after death. For when the body is no longer fit to receive the projected power of soul, we must then ask what happens to that power. Plotinus had faced the same problem but without giving a very clear answer. For him these powers of soul are dissipated in the universe as a whole.[6] But Porphyry was more interested in the so-called 'irrational powers' of soul as part of the human being. And this interest in the lower soul is not unconnected with his concern to promote the well-being of the average man that we have found in his attitude to religious cults. While the philosopher may succeed in cutting himself off entirely from the body on death, most men continue this relationship even after death because their souls have not freed themselves from entanglement with the passions during their earthly life. The *pneuma* supplies the substrate for the continued activity of the irrational soul and it is this lower soul that is the focus for the purification after death of those who have not lived a fully moral or philosophical life. This then can be linked to the traditional punishments of the underworld.[7]

Other Plotinian themes which occur in the *Sententiae* include the stress on the active as opposed to the passive role of the soul in perception,[8] the unaffectability of the soul,[9] the unity of intellect and intelligible. And very importantly the themes include the stress on power as not being dependent on bulk and the relative powerlessness of bulk,[10] ideas which strongly influenced Augustine, whether taken from Plotinus himself or from Porphyry. Another idea, which though based on Plotinus, was to become a universally applied formula, was the general principle that

> everything is present in everything else, but in the manner appropriate to the being of each level. For everything is in intellect intellectually, in soul rationally, in plants seminally, in bodies formally, in the transcendent in a manner not intelligible and beyond being.[11]

Plotinus had used the concept to reconcile the variety and unity of Intellect:

> Each there has everything in itself and sees all things in every other, so that all are everywhere and each and every one is all and the glory is unbounded ... A different kind of being stands out in each, but in each all are manifest.[12]

The idea was extensively used by Iamblichus as a means of linking and unifying the variety of levels of being. Proclus, too, makes use of it and applied it in *The Elements of Theology* to the unity of Being, Life and Intelligence in the second Hypostasis:

> All things are in all things, but in each according to its proper nature: for in Being there is life and intellect; in Life, being and intellect; in Intellect, being and life; but each of

> these exists upon one level intellectually, upon another vitally, and on the third existentially.[13]

This is a good example of how an idea becomes formalised over time until it becomes a concise and coherently expressed universal principle. While it is certainly not true that later Neoplatonists did not develop new and philosophically valuable theories of their own, they also accepted the basic structure bequeathed to them by Plotinus and transmitted to them overlaid with Porphyry's systematising analysis.

THE LATER NEOPLATONISTS – IAMBLICHUS AND PROCLUS

Whether Iamblichus was ever a formal pupil of Porphyry is difficult to say, but he is responsible for bringing Neoplatonism to the Eastern part of the Roman world. Just how it came about that Neoplatonism became the standard form of Platonism is difficult to say. Plutarch (died 432) is the first Neoplatonist we know of as formal head of the Academy in Athens. He was succeeded by Syrianus (died *c*.437) and his more famous pupil Proclus (412–485).

One of the first things we notice about these later Neoplatonists is the format of their 'published' work, which tends to take the form of commentaries, mostly on Plato. We do have from Proclus a very illuminating handbook of Neoplatonic metaphysics, *The Elements of Theology*, which deals with the One, Intellect and Soul. But in general their ideas are expressed through the published versions of the reading courses which they established for their students.

Courses

The basic outline of courses in the Neoplatonic schools was probably already established by the time of Iamblichus. Study commenced with the logical works of Aristotle. Plato's dialogues were then introduced in a series of cycles. Introductory material was provided by the *Alcibides, Gorgias* and *Phaedo,* which were read for their 'ethical' content. These were followed by the *Cratylus* and *Theaetetus* which provided an introduction to Platonic logic. The *Sophist* and *Statesman* were considered as introductions to the physical world, the Sophist being regarded as the creator of the sublunary world and the myth of the *Statesman* providing a Zeus who could be seen as the demiurge. The *Phaedrus* and *Symposium* were the introduction to theology. This cycle was finally completed with the *Philebus* which introduced the highest principles with the unlimited and limit. The whole course then culminated in the reading of the *Timaeus* and *Parmenides* which summed up the two main divisions of the Neoplatonic world, the *Timaeus* presenting the definitive Platonic view of the physical universe, the *Parmenides* the ultimate delineation of the transcendent world. A curious omission is the *Republic*, whose central portion with the Sun, Line and Cave analogies was so important for the Neoplatonists. But even though sections of the *Republic,* and of the *Laws,* were fundamental to Neoplatonic metaphysics, the texts themselves were probably too long and too full of less relevant material to make them suitable for lecture purposes. We might also add that the Chaldaean Oracles were also the subject of lengthy commentaries which suggests that they may have been taught to special groups. Rhetoric was also taught in the Academy under Proclus where it served as an introduction to logic and probably appealed to a larger number of students who did not go on to take the philosophy courses. The way in which all of this impinges on us is that many of the surviving works of the later Neoplatonists are in commentary form and that too sometimes as lecture notes of a pupil.

Transcendence of the One

One of the most radical ideas proposed by Plotinus was a first principle that was utterly transcendent. We have already refered to the reasons why Plotinus proposed such a first principle and also to some of the difficulties involved in maintaining it. His successors, paradoxically, both exaggerated and weakened this transcendence in an attempt to deal with the problems it entailed. Already in Porphyry we can see a tendency to attempt to create a stronger link between the One and Intellect. He appears to do this by exploiting the triadic idea already implicitly expressed in Plotinus himself.[14] Although strictly there are only two levels of reality at issue here, the One and Intellect, even Plotinus had at times suggested a sort of transitional phase characterised as a yet undefined power going forth from the One. This could be identified with the Indefinite Dyad. The idea of a threefold relationship is an attractive one as it can express a starting and final point mediated through a third element. If we now add to this the notion of effect prefigured in the cause, we could say that the One already contains implicitly its effects, the outgoing power and Intellect. In reverse we could maintain that the effect contains or implies the causes and so Intellect in this sense contains the One and the outgoing power. It remains only to do the same with the outgoing power which can be said to imply its cause, the One, and its effect, Intellect. We thus produce the following series of relationships, which are an expression of the general principle that everything is in everything in a way appropriate to the particular level:

One	*Power*	*Intellect*
One	Power	*Intellect*
One	*Power*	**Intellect**

It would seem that Porphyry produced a scheme of this kind. It must be stressed that there was no intention here to hypostasise any of these elements other than the first and the last, the One and Intellect. A further elaboration, which strengthens the link between the One and Intellect, may be found in an anonymous commentary on Plato's *Parmenides,* which some scholars attribute to Porphyry.[15] Here the notion of existence (*hyparxis)* is introduced into the nature of the One. This provides a link with Intellect when Intellect is considered under the aspect of Being. A more complex and systematic version appears in Victorinus and was exploited by him to express Christian Trinitarian ideas. In fact we can also trace here the development of the subsequently important distinction between existence and substance, to be and to be something. This development, whether due to Porphyry or to some unknown 'successor', represented a profound move away from Plotinus who adamantly denied any notion of being or even existence to the One.

The exploitation of triads was to lead to even greater elaboration in subsequent Neoplatonic metaphysics. For the moment, however, we will restrict our view to the problem of the One. It would appear that Iamblichus and Proclus thought that Porphyry's schema actually demoted the One rather than solved the question of its transcendence. It may be in this context that Iamblichus felt obliged to posit an even loftier first principle, which he called the 'Ineffable'[16] and which he placed above the One of Porphyry and Plotinus. Perhaps, like Damascius later, he felt that the very name 'one' implied a relationship with plurality which compromised the purity and absoluteness of the highest principle. The idea was rejected by Proclus who, as we will see, preferred to find a solution for the One's absolute nature without postulating a higher principle.

Most importantly Proclus stressed even more than Plotinus the transcendence of the One in negative terms. This transcendence is given even greater prominence by extending to Intellect what seem in Plotinus to be the marks of the One itself:

> For the transcendent One-Being is truly a revered object, as ensconced in unity; it is great, as possessing an incomprehensible power, and secret, as remaining inexpressible and inscrutable at the summit of existence.[17]

The greater remoteness of Intellect had profound repercussions for the individual soul as we will see later, but it also formed an aspect of Proclus' increasingly strict apophatic approach to the One. Even the terms 'maker', 'father' and 'divine' are denied. It is only by negation that we can speak of the One at all. And yet negation leads, positively we might say, to a revealing of or rather a pointing towards the overriding power of the One. In a careful and systematic examination of negation Proclus suggests that there is a kind of negation which is superior to assertion.[18] This is the kind of negation which is made of non-being which is above being, as opposed to negations made of what has being. Assertions tend to analyse into parts, negations to simplify. Nor is negation as applied to the One a kind of privation (*steresis*), for the One is not deprived of anything that it might have, for although the One is the cause of everything, it itself is none of the things of which it is the cause. Moreover for this very reason it is the cause of the assertions derived from the negations made of it.

> So then not even in this sense are the negations uttered of the One; for the One does not come to be in any one thing, but although it is the cause of the assertions of which we apply to it the negations, it in no way comes to be in those things of which it is the cause.[19]

In this way assertion is neatly linked causally to negation without in any way diminishing the cause by predicating attributes of it. Furthermore the ineffability of the One is not simply the result of our own inadequacies but is due to the very nature of the One itself. The One is utterly unknowable; neither the soul, nor even Intellect can 'know' the One. But since they are dependent on it and by this dependence are always striving towards it, they can strive to be like the One. In the end even negations do not apply strictly to the One itself but point towards it in the sense of being a kind of preparation for the final ascent to likeness with it:

> For, if we are to approach the One by means of these negative conceptions and to emancipate ourselves from our accustomed ways of thought, we must strip off the variety of life and remove our multifarious concerns, and render the soul alone by itself, and thus expose it to the divine and to the reception of divinely inspired power in order that having first lived in such a way as to deny the multiplicity within ourselves, we may thus ascend to the undifferentiated intuition of the One.[20]

This way of approaching the One is not simply conceptual, but the culmination of a way of life; it is not simply thought, but thought and experience. Since negation has brought us only so far as to point to the One, which itself lies beyond, the final logical step is to negate the negations; i.e. to let go of the negations as positive pointers, so as to continue the encounter beyond *all* discourse, in what Proclus calls 'silence'. If we have strayed now beyond strict metaphysics into the realm of individual experience, that is only proper, since purely conceptual analysis cannot be separated, particularly at the higher levels of reality, from the experience of reality. Neoplatonic dialectic is both conceptual and experiential. When it comes to the One the way of negation (apophasis) is not simply a way of abstraction in the Aristotelian sense. Apophasis is a form of purification.

Procession, return and triads – formalisation of metaphysical relationships

In many ways the use of the triadic concept to explore and express relationships may appear a quite natural mode of human cognition. It is used, for example, by Hegel, though his triad of thesis–antithesis–synthesis is somewhat different from those of the Neoplatonists, even though he was influenced by the thought of Proclus. We may, however, find its profuse application by the Neoplatonists disconcerting and at times over-formalised and sterile. There is one further point to bear in mind; Iamblichus and Proclus show a distinct tendency to endow every distinction which the human mind conceives with an objective and independent metaphysical existence. And so for them, unlike Plotinus and Porphyry, the mid-term acquires an independent reality. This applies in other cases, too; for example, 'eternity', which for Porphyry and Plotinus is a mode of reality, becomes a sort of hypostasis in itself. This had the added advantage that such entities could be identified with and thus account for the multitude of divine beings to be encountered in the religious traditions of the age: in this case *Aion* could be identified as the god of eternity. This tendency to make every logical distinction into an ontological one led to the rather rigid formalisation of the priority of Being over thinking. As we have already seen,[21] Plotinus had dealt with this issue in a flexible way; sometimes placing Being after Thinking, but always adverting to the fact that there is no question here of temporal priority and noting the inadequacy of our discursive reason to rise above the level of the distinctions it is forced to make because of its own nature. Iamblichus and Proclus, however, wanted to make much clearer distinctions and, allied with their general tendency to objectify all concepts, very firmly held that Being precedes Intellect. This then led to a clear distinction within the second Hypostasis between a higher level of Intelligibles, objects of thought existing independently of thinking and identifiable with Being, and a lower level, which they called the Intellectual, which denotes active thinking. In order to link the two it remained only to posit a mid-term, Intelligible and Intellectual. This triad was also associated with another: Being–Life–Thought, a combination which we have already seen in Porphyry and which may be found in Plotinus. Behind this triad lies the very rich concept employed by Plotinus of 'activity', the equivalent of 'life', as the linking agent which enabled him to identify Being with Thinking.[22] This comparison with Plotinus allows us to dispel the sometimes rather arid-seeming formalism of later Neoplatonism and to see the significance of their mode of philosophising. For they are dealing with the same difficult metaphysical issues as Plotinus, but trying to explicate them in a way which they consider to be more precise. If their solutions seem over-rigid and often over-complex and their multiplication of entities seems to lead to a distancing of entities from each other rather than their integration, this in the end may come down to a question of philosophical style, both in ourselves and in the Neoplatonists, rather than being one of essential difference. Of course such differences of 'style' did lead to some quite profoundly different doctrinal conclusions.

But before considering these we will look at some other complementary developments, in all of which we will be able to see the same tendency to make ever further distinctions in order to bridge the gap between entities. The later Neoplatonists identified ontological and hierarchical distinctions even within the broad levels to which we have already referred. For example to account for the relationship of Intellect to the many individual intellects they identify Intellect itself as the Monad or source of the many intellects which are at a lower level and are themselves further organised on a descending scale. These are referred to as a series (*seira*). The same applies to Soul with its *seira* of individual souls. In this way the identity of Soul and souls, Intellect and intellects, so carefully and ingeniously argued for in Plotinus is compromised, and the individual intellect and soul is demoted in the hierarchy. Indeed, as we will see later, the intellect of the individual human is demoted even further by being regarded as a mere reflection (*ellampsis*) of an intellect in the soul. Proclus took this concept even further by positing a seira for the One, whose members are termed *henads* after *hen,* the Greek for One. These he could then identify with the highest rank of gods.[23] The principle of Monads and their series is expressed succinctly by him:

> Since then in every order there is some common element, a continuity and identity in virtue of which some things are said to be co-ordinate and others not, it is apparent that the identical element is derived by the whole order from a single originative principle.[24]

It is the single originative principle that makes, for example, all intellects intellects and all souls souls, while each soul has its own peculiar properties that make it an individual. In the same way each intellect represents a particular Form while Intellect may be said to be all intellects and thus all Forms by virtue of its uniting role as Monad. The same issue appears in Plotinus when he discusses the problem of how a horse, an irrational being, can be derived from an intellect.[25] One of the arguments he briefly alludes to is that there are hierarchical differences even in Intellect:

> There must be degrees of brightness and clearness, first, second and third according to their nearness to the first principles. So some thoughts are gods, others of a second kind, to which belongs what we call rationality here, and below these comes what is called the irrational.[26]

A related concept is the distinction between *participated* and *unparticipated* Forms. The problem of how the Forms, which are universal, are participated by particulars is raised by Plato himself in the first part of the *Parmenides.* In his solution of this issue Proclus identifies three levels: that which participates – in this case the body; that which is participated – the universal form; and that which is unparticipated – the transcendent form. The last is therefore unaffected by the participant and its integrity preserved, while the participated universal can provide the necessary link with the participating body. The principle is then applied in a much wider way to the relationship of Hypostases with each other. Thus Intellect is unparticipated and transcendent, while intellects are participated by soul, and Soul is unparticipated while souls are participated by bodies. Above all the One is unparticipated while the henads provide the universals which can be participated, in the first instance by intellects. The idea is further developed by Proclus in a way that can provide a chain of participation from an individual henad to an individual intellect, soul and body. Moreover, as we shall see, since the higher principles are more powerful and their influence spreads more widely, a henad may be directly participated by a particular body.

Finally the concept of the *self-constituted* formalised and developed another idea basic to Plotinus and, in a sense, also to Plato. The idea that the soul was 'self-moved' was essential to the Platonic theory of the nature of the soul as an immortal entity (*Phaedrus* 245–246). This idea was adopted by Plotinus as a key argument for the immortality of the soul[27] and found its way into the Western tradition through Augustine. But its application was wider. Each Hypostasis after the One was dependent on the One, but also dependent on itself for its final formation, i.e. both in its movement from its producer and, more particularly, in its movement back in contemplation of its producer, a movement which secured its perfection. Thus the idea of self-constitution, though not formally expressed by a fixed term, may already be found in Plotinus. In Proclus it becomes a key concept which, for example, helps to stress the natural immortality of the soul, a fundamental difference with the orthodox Christian view of the soul which makes its immortality dependent on God. However in Iamblichus and Proclus the concept of 'self-constitution' tends to place greater emphasis on the independent reality of each substance than did the nascent idea in Plotinus and Porphyry.

The presence of the One

Although for Plotinus the One is the cause of all unity in the cosmos, its presence at times seems rather remote and mediated through Intellect and Soul. Indeed in his treatise on the omnipresence of Being[28] in which he grapples with the difficult problem of how incorporeals are present to corporeals he does not mention the One at all but is satisfied with speaking more generally of Being. But Proclus gives more emphasis to the Plotinian idea that the higher a Hypostasis is in the hierachy the more powerful it is, in order to show that the effects of the One must be more extensive than those of Intellect, and those of Intellect more so than those of Soul. This may be illustrated by the faculties of soul which are not all present to all things in the cosmos, whereas every single thing that is must share in unity if it is to exist at all. But even these must have Being. Proclus now goes further and, taking that which does not have Being, namely matter, links it causally with the One, thus clarifying an issue that had been left unresolved by Plotinus.[29]

> From this[30] it is apparent that what Soul causes is caused also by Intellect, but not all that Intellect causes is caused by Soul. Intellect operates prior to Soul and what Soul bestows on secondary existences Intellect bestows in greater measure, and at a level where Soul is no longer operative Intellect irradiates with its own gifts things on which Soul has not bestowed itself. For even the inanimate participates Intellect, or the creative activity of intellect, in so far as it participates Form. Moreover what Intellect causes is also caused by the Good, but not conversely. For even privation of Form is from the Good, since it is the source of all things, but Intellect, being Form, cannot give rise to privation.[31]

This theory of the generation of matter is a strikingly clear avoidance of the ambiguity found in Plotinus who did not feel prepared to state so positively that the One is the cause of matter. Here Proclus agrees with his master Syrianus who had already accepted the Aristotelian criticism of Plato that there can be no Forms of negations.[32]

Besides removing a possible dualism from the system, Proclus' concept of linking diminishing power with increasing complexity produced a metaphysical structure which displayed its maximum complexity at the level of the human soul, while beneath this the reverse is the case as each lower level of reality shows an increasing simplicity until we finally come down to matter. The importance of this idea may be seen in the fact that it was adopted by Aquinas[33] in order to make matter (the prime matter of Aristotle) a creation of god.

Of course in this lower half of the structure of the universe there is a decrease of power. Yet since what is lowest shares more exclusively in the attributes of the One, there is a sense in which we can say that it is closer. This led to two further corollaries. The causal presence of the One was closer to the whole of the natural world and therefore divine immanence could be expressed more powerfully. This was an idea that was to become immensely important in the philosophy of the Middle Ages as transmitted through the Arabic *Liber de causis*. Second it provided a theoretical grounding for theurgy since a simple stone could be linked directly through a henad to the One itself.[34]

Evil

Proclus' clear statement that matter is a product of the One meant that it could no longer be identified with evil, since then evil would be a product of the One. It was, however, axiomatic that evil is not due to god.[35] The solution was to make evil simply the absence of good with no existence of its own. In any case evil is not found in the universe as a whole but only in its parts and can *sub specie aeternitatis* lead to good. The latter is a traditional argument that can be found among the Stoics and was also put forward by Plotinus, but the denial of existence to evil solved the dangerous ambiguity of Plotinus who seemed to give evil as identified with matter an active power of distortion.

The status of the individual soul

Iamblichus and Proclus seem to have demoted the human soul and to have abandoned the optimism of Plotinus that the individual can attain continuous contemplation of the Intelligible world in this life. This direction seems to have been influenced by their general tendency to emphasise the independence of Hypostases. And in their attempt to show the continuity of the chain of causation by the creation of ever further distinct levels the effect was rather to increase the gaps between the major realities. Thus whereas Plotinus had placed only the activities of the individual soul and the World Soul in time, they considered all the activities of Soul to be in time.

And so when faced, as Plotinus had been, with the observation that humans only intermittently exercise reason or show contact with the Intelligible world, their response was to draw a distinction between different levels of soul. Human souls think intermittently and it is the divine souls that are always thinking, though in time; for it is only intellects that think eternally. Now while it is true that for Plotinus it is not precisely the soul which thinks in the full sense of the term, there is nevertheless an intimate connection between the soul of each individual and the intellect of each individual, so much so that Plotinus can express this by declaring that a part of the soul has never ceased to have the experience of contact with its intellect. In this way he provides the means for the individual to reclaim even in his earthly life the experience of living at the level of Intellect. But Iamblichus and Proclus vehemently denied the notion of an undescended part of the soul. For them the link between individual soul and intellect is less close. In fact if the lower orders are always more numerous than the higher then it follows that some souls, namely human souls, will not have an individual intellect.[36] Allied with this demotion of the hierarchical status of the individual soul was a greater concern with the soul's susceptibility to being affected by the external world, expressed in the notion that the soul, if corrupted by external contact, somehow changes in essence, a turn of phrase which Plotinus would have avoided. This reduced status of the individual soul was then complemented by the increased role of religious ritual (including theurgy) in the life of these philosophers. This combination of philosophy and religion proved to be both an inspiration and a difficulty for Christian thinkers as we will see in the next chapter.

8

CHRISTIANITY AND NEOPLATONISM

There can be no doubt about the important influence of the Neoplatonists on Christian thinkers and theologians, an influence which continued long after the end of antiquity. As an introduction to the way in which Neoplatonism influenced Christian thought it is instructive to begin with two quite different individuals, Synesius, a Greek from the Eastern part of the Roman Empire, and Augustine, a Latin speaker from the West. Although both were bishops their concerns differed.

Synesius

Synesius (370–413) could trace his family back to the earliest Doric aristocracy of Cyrene, a Greek colony founded in the seventh century BC near the coast of North Africa in present-day Libya. He was clearly a person of independent means and his study of philosophy in Alexandria with Hypatia was part of the education of a gentleman. On his return to his native Cyrene he looked after his estates, enjoyed hunting and writing, and, as was expected of a man of his means, took part in local civic administration, including a deputation to Constantinople. Synesius was a convert to Christianity, but just when he became a Christian is difficult to say. He had already established a family when he was asked by the Metropolitan of Alexandria to become bishop of Cyrene and the Pentapolis. This momentous step which involved his being baptised, ordained and consecrated bishop all at once, was not taken lightly by Synesius; some of his reservations are revealed in a letter to his brother.[1] Apart from not wanting to be parted from his wife and family, he formulates three major doctrinal issues which stood in his way, for he evidently did not want to abandon his Platonism: the creation of the individual soul by god at the moment of incarnation, the final dissolution of the physical universe and the resurrection:

> It is difficult, if not impossible, for doctrines to be shaken which have entered the soul through knowledge and proof. You know that philosophy in many ways opposes these doctrines that are on everyone's lips. To be sure, I will never think it right to consider the soul to be generated after the body. I will not say that the cosmos and its parts will perish. The resurrection that everyone speaks about I consider to be something sacred and inexpressible and I am far from agreeing with the ideas held by the masses.

The Platonic counterparts of these doctrines were fundamental and often repeated. The eternity of the universe was taken for granted by almost all Greek philosophers and would have seemed a perfectly logical view to hold. It is its opposite that creates difficulties. The Neoplatonic acceptence of the pre-existence of the soul is supported primarily from arguments in the *Phaedo* and is basic to the notion of the soul's immortality, while the resurrection, whether of Christ or of the individual body, is an idea that runs counter to the Platonic teaching that we must 'flee the body' and try to separate the soul from the body as much as possible, in preparation for the final separation that comes with the death of our bodies. In fact according to the Neoplatonists only the impure keep their individual bodies after death; for they retain a lingering physical presence around their souls which prevents them from attaining complete union with the divine. Despite the fact that the world always exists and soul is always giving life to the world and that even the individual soul contributes to the life of the universe, a doctrine we have seen in Plotinus, the counter-striving for freedom from the body exerts itself even more powerfully. In the end, for the Platonist the individual body is not part of a man's identity and its retention is an encumbrance rather than a vindication of its value.

That the pre-existence of the soul is as inevitable as its continued existence after departure from the body is basic to the notion of the nature of soul as self-moving. Only if it does not possess the cause of existence outside itself can it be immortal. Popular handbooks of Neoplatonism, such as that by Sallustius, repeat the idea, with the additional argument that souls must come back at some stage into bodies, otherwise the world would eventually become depopulated, since new souls cannot be created.[2] We should note that for

Neoplatonists, even if all souls are dependent causally on Intellect, this dependence is an eternal one which does not affect the basic self-moving nature of soul.

The eternity of the universe is another idea which is fundamental to the whole of Neoplatonic metaphysics. For if the world ceased to exist, that which caused it must also cease to exist, which is impossible. The argument is based on the nature of the primary cause; it does not choose to act, but always acts productively; its activity is its essence. Thus for a Platonist the rejection of the eternity of the universe is an attack on the nature of the divine cause itself.

The defence of the Platonic position was taken up by Proclus[3] who was in turn criticised by Johannes Philoponus (490–570),[4] an Alexandrian Christian who wrote commentaries on Aristotle and who published his work against Proclus in the same year (529) that Justinian 'closed' the philosophical schools in Athens.[5] Elements of this debate are also to be found in the works of Aeneas of Gaza. In fact both Philoponus and Aeneas (who later became bishop of Mytilene) had been pupils in Alexandria of the pagan philosopher Ammonius.[6] His other pupils had included Damascius, the last head of the Athenian Academy and his colleague Simplicius. There seems to have been a much easier relationship between pagans and Christians in the Alexandrian schools than the rather hostile situation which is found in Athens.[7] And it seems likely that Ammonius came to some kind of understanding with the Christian authorities whereby teaching continued in his school, possibly by agreeing not to lay too much stress on philosophical support for pagan religious ritual, in particular theurgy.[8] On the question of the eternity of the universe Philoponus not only tried to refute the arguments of Proclus but also attempted to present a positive argument for a temporal beginning of the universe. In fact the logic of the pagan position had sometimes been recognised. Basil, for example, seems to accept that reason leads us to suppose an eternal universe, but that this view must then be corrected by revelation.[9] Philoponus' positive argument is based on the exploitation of the notion that time is infinitely divisible, an idea used since Aristotle as a component of one argument for the eternity of the universe; if time is infinite, there will never be a beginning point to past time nor an end point to future time. Philoponus' argument is that this kind of infinity can only be an actual one, that is in fact experienced by finite individuals as a whole, and so, however many intermediate points there may be, the whole is finite and thus has beginning and end. Although this argument is used subsequently by both Islamic and Christian thinkers it did not settle the issue. Some of the other arguments for an eternal universe evinced interesting and constructive ripostes, though again without a final solution to the debate. It will suffice to mention two main types of argument: those that are based on the changelessness of the divine cause and those that ask the question 'why did the universe begin now and not later?'

The idea that god or the ultimate cause of the universe is changeless can be traced back to the Presocratics[10] and to Plato[11] who adds that any change in the supreme and best must be a change to the worse which is inadmissible. The argument may centre on a number of aspects: the causal nature of the divine, the sufficiency of the cause, or god's will. In each case it appears that some kind of change is suggested in the cause. In the case of pure cause it seems that god has altered his state from not causing to causing, in that of sufficiency that he is at one moment unable to cause and at the next able to cause, and in that of will that he moves to a state of willing a world from one of not willing it. The last is neatly parried by Augustine who points to the difference between changing one's will and willing a change.[12] The question as to what god was doing before he created the world (was he doing nothing?) which involves the same basic issue as the question of why the world began at this rather than that point of time, is also answered by Augustine with the denial that time existed 'before' creation.

THE WESTERN TRADITION

The fact that Plotinus and Porphyry were active in Rome must have made an enormous contribution to the spread of their ideas in the Western part of the Roman Empire. The works of Plotinus and Porphyry were readily accessible in the Greek-speaking East from the very beginning. But it seems likely that influence from the East reached the West less easily than the reverse, although Boethius in the early sixth century seems to have known some of the work of Proclus and may well have visited Alexandria. Nevertheless in general it was the work of Plotinus and Porphyry that was to be of primary importance for Western Christians. Porphyry, who had been responsible for publishing a definitive text of the works of Plotinus, which he entitled the *Enneads*, had also written commentaries on Plotinus' treatises and, in general, made his thought more accessible to newcomers. It is often difficult to know whether Western readers in particular were taking their ideas from Porphyry or from Plotinus himself. There is still an argument as to whether Augustine, for example, had read Plotinus himself. It is impossible to decide and perhaps not so important. Augustine probably would have read Greek philosophical texts for the most part in Latin translations and may well have encountered the words of Plotinus in an anthology or in Porphyry's commentaries which probably contained extensive quotations. It is Augustine who will mostly concern us here, because of the immense importance of his works for subsequent Western theologians and thinkers. And our concentration will be on those ideas where he owes most to the influence of the Neoplatonists. But Augustine would also have owed a great deal either directly or indirectly to Marius Victorinus who not only translated the works of Plotinus and Porphyry but was profoundly influenced by them *particularly* in his speculations on the Trinity.

Marius Victorinus

Victorinus was a convert to Christianity very late in life. He had been a very successful teacher of rhetoric in Rome, even to the extent of having a statue erected to himself in the Forum of Trajan. Augustine, who had been reading Victorinus' translations of the 'books of the Platonists', recounts in his *Confessions* the story of Victorinus' conversion as told by his mentor Simplicianus, who further recommends to him the Platonists in whose works he claims God and his Son are implied.[13] In fact Victorinus was inspired precisely by the Neoplatonic Hypostases of the One and Intellect in his complex trinitarian theology which he published after his conversion. His chief concern was to provide a defence of the Nicean trinitarian doctrine which made the Father and the Son consubstantial (*homoousios*). The Neoplatonic speculation which most influenced him in this enterprise was their thinking on the relationship of the One and Intellect. Victorinus accepted the absolute transcendence of the Father as being like that of the One, beyond being and beyond knowledge. The Son, as Logos, is also the manifestation or image of the Father. So far the transcendent One of Plotinus served well to differentiate Father from Son, but since they must equally be of one substance Victorinus exploited the ideas of Porphyry in which the closeness of the two Hypostases, the One and Intellect, were emphasised. Porphyry had developed a schema of triple triads to help to explain how power and intellect are prefigured transcendentally in the One, how power also contains unity and intellect and the resultant Intellect contains unity and power, which can also be termed 'life'. By identifying the Father as the One, the Son as Life and the Holy Spirit as Intellect, all three could be regarded as being of one substance since each implied the other and could yet be manifested individually just as Life and Intellect are predominant in their own triads. Victorinus also made use of two further Neoplatonic principles: that each level of reality remains unaffected when engendering a further (subordinate) reality and the notion of independence which Plotinus had suggested by his *tolma* and which appeared in the later Neoplatonic notion of the 'self-generated' or *authupostaton.* By using both of these Victorinus could express the self-generation of the Son and maintain the integrity of each person of the Trinity in the causal act. But just as interesting as the actual application of philosophical ideas to his completed trinitarian doctrines is Victorinus' method. In both of the works in which he gives the fullest account of his trinitarian ideas he is primarily concerned to combat the doctrines of Arianism and in particular to demonstrate how the Son can be different from the Father and yet of the same substance. These works, however, include more philosophical material than is necessary for his case, for in each there are long passages of an almost purely philosophical rather than theological or scriptural character which tease out the ideas that he will then apply to the theological problem. But they often contain ideas which, though part of the philosophical complex, are not at all relevant to his immediate needs. It is here that we have an insight into the working mind of the Neoplatonist turned Christian theologian and into some of the philosophical sources on which he nurtured his speculations, sources which probably go back to Porphyry but which may well have been developed further in the intervening years.[14]

Augustine

Augustine himself chronicles for us the influence of Neoplatonism on his philosophical and spiritual development. As he matured in his thought he came to reject and modify some of the Neoplatonic ideas which he had accepted all too readily at the moment when he first encountered them. Although he is familiar with the earlier tradition of Platonism and knows of Apuleius, who like himself was from North Africa, he mentions Plotinus, Porphyry and Iamblichus as the most important of the 'modern' philosophers[15] and acknowledges

Plotinus as the philosopher who was considered to 'have understood Plato more thoroughly than anyone else, at any rate in modern times'.[16] He himself speaks of the profound influence of this encounter with the 'books of the Platonists':

> By reading these books of the Platonists I had been prompted to look for truth as something incorporeal, and I 'caught sight of your invisible nature, as it is known through your creatures' (*Rom.* 1.20). Though I was thwarted of my wish to know more, I was conscious of what it was that my mind was too clouded to see. I was certain both that you are and that you are infinite, though without extent in terms of space either limited or unlimited.[17]

Concept of incorporeal Being

Perhaps the most profound and lasting impact was made by their concept of incorporeal being. Augustine had become deeply embroiled in Manicheism, a quasi-christian religious sect which held a strongly materialist view of reality. Plotinus himself had endlessly combated the hold of materialist thought which must have been more widespread at the time than we sometimes suppose. After all, the Stoics whose thought was still influential in the time of Plotinus held what was in the end a materialist view of the nature of god and the soul. Such a view was extremely problematical for a Christian concept of god and in particular raised the difficult problem of god being affected from outside himself. But it was equally difficult to show how there could be any kind of causal relationship between a physical body and an incorporeal entity. These were problems which, we have already seen, occupied Plotinus from many different viewpoints.

The nature of the incorporeal is the chief focus of Augustine's work *On the Magnitude of the Soul* (*de quantitate animae*) in which he seeks to show that the soul is not a physical entity and how an incorporeal entity can relate to a physical body. The very title of the work is provocative, for the kind of magnitude that the reader is first led to expect is a physical one, whereas Augustine's aim is to demonstrate the magnitude of the incorporeal power of the soul. It is an ambiguity with which both Plotinus and Porphyry had played.[18] Augustine rejects the notion of physical size in the case of the soul:

> The soul must not be regarded in any way as either long, or wide, or strong. Such qualities, in my opinion, are attributes of bodies; thus we are merely applying to the soul our ideas about bodies.[19]

But given this hypothesis it must first be shown that if the soul is not body it is not nothing. He must then demonstrate how an incorporeal power relates to the physical body. The first is approached by looking at instances of realities which are not corporeal but have a kind of existence. His first example, 'justice', has clearly Platonic origins. He then adverts to the power of memory in language that reminds us of his later discussion of this topic in the *Confessions* where memory is central to his concept of the human soul.

> I wish you to consider somewhat more carefully how great and how many objects our memory contains; all of these, of course, are contained in the soul. How great therefore, the depth, the width, the immensity of the soul that can hold all these things.[20]

The concentration on memory as the central faculty of the human soul, while doubtless owing much to the Platonic notion of recollection and the Plotinian discursive reason, is primarily due to Augustine's own reflection on the powers of his own inner self. There is a sense in which the whole of the *Confessions,* as the biography of a spiritual search, is centred on memory: both memory of the personal past and memory or recalling of the god who was never absent. After the appeal to memory Augustine takes us into the abstract values of geometry, the main purpose of which is to demonstrate that these are realities which are not corporeal and that the soul which thinks them cannot itself be corporeal. Again we are reminded of the Platonic positioning of geometricals as superior to physical bodies and as pointing towards pure forms. Augustine then concludes that the soul which contemplates geometrical values must be in fact greater than them. Having shown that the soul is an incorporeal power, he must now attempt to demonstrate more precisely what kind of power it is and how it is related to the body. The soul is linked with growth in the body and more importantly with the rational powers excercised through the body. Of these perception presents the most acute problems when focusing on the soul–body relationship, just as it had done for Plotinus. Like Plotinus, Augustine is anxious to show that the object of sensation does not in any way affect the incorporeal soul in a physical manner. This is achieved, again in a way reminiscent of Plotinus, by distinguishing sensation from perception and by stressing the active power of the soul in perception. The human soul also has reason which is a mark of man's superiority to animals for whom the level of sense-perception is their 'reason'.

> But because reason and knowledge, of which we are treating now, transcend the senses, the human soul by means of reason and knowledge withdraws itself as far as it can from the body and gladly enjoys the delights of the interior life. The more it stoops to the senses, the greater is its similarity to the brute.[21]

The Neoplatonic emphasis on withdrawing from the body and looking inwards to the life of reason is obvious here. More important is the way in which this leads Augustine to exhort us to bring back our souls to god.

> Therefore, although this is a digression, I am happy to emphasise the good advice that the soul should not pour itself out in the senses beyond the measure of necessity, but rather should recall itself from the senses and become a child of God again, that is, be made a new man by putting off the old.[22]

Although he calls this a digression from the strict philosophical theme of the work, the return of the soul is in fact the true purpose and end of the enquiry about the nature of the soul, something which is made clear in the final chapter which describes the stages of the soul's ascent. This is, as with Plotinus, a combination of spiritual experience and rigorous philosophical enquiry – 'study with a sense of reverence'.[23]

Another aspect of Augustine's discovery of the concept of incorporeality is the realisation that the human too has this incorporeal dimension as the most important part of his being. There is no better introduction to Augustine's grasp of the nature and importance of the interior man than his own discussion of the search within the self as it is expressed in Book Ten of the *Confessions*. As Plotinus did in *Enneads* V.1, Augustine conducts the enquiry about the nature of the macrocosm – in this case the search for god – by an introspection into the many layers of the human being. This search combines strict analysis of the nature of the human soul with a profound awareness of the element of personal experience. It is this combination of reason and experience so central to the spirit of Plotinus, and we might say to all Neoplatonism, that probably appealed most to Augustine.

To answer the question 'what is my god?' Augustine turns within himself in the realisation that he consists of an inner and outer persona:

> Then I turned to myself and asked, 'Who are you?' 'A man,' I replied. But it is clear that I have both body and soul, the one the outer, the other the inner part of me.[24]

The first inner powers to be identified are those that give life to the body and above these the powers that govern our ability to perceive the world around us. But even animals possess these powers. Augustine now comes to what he sees as the central and most important human faculty, that of memory, which he identifies with the mind itself. His analysis of memory is one of the most sustained passages of philosophical reflection in the *Confessions.* In it he displays a determination to reach a full understanding and at the same time a sense of wonder and stimulating puzzlement at the problems the concept presents. We might recall that Plato, too, had regarded 'wonder' as the starting point of philosophising.[25] This is how Augustine expresses it in the midst of his enquiry.

> I am lost in wonder when I consider this problem. It bewilders me. Yet men go out and gaze in astonishment at high mountains, the huge waves of the sea, the broad reaches of rivers, the ocean that encircles the world, or the stars in their courses. But they pay no attention to themselves.[26]

He begins by noting the power of the memory to store sensations derived from different senses and yet keep them separate. We can isolate the different categories and work with them separately if we wish; sound, colour, tastes, tactile qualities, are each supplied by distinct senses, hearing, vision, taste, touch. Furthermore we can recall sensations when the actual sensation has ceased, a sight when what we saw has long since passed from our vision, or music can be recalled in our mind without the accompaniment of any physical sound or the intervention of sense-images from different sources:

> I can sing as much as I want, even though my tongue does not move and my throat utters no sound. And when I recall into my mind this rich reserve of sound, which entered my memory through my ears, the images of colour, which are also there in my memory, do not interfere or intrude.[27]

But all of these memories are of sense-objects, that is, of impressions or images which remain when the objects themselves have disappeared. There are other kinds of memories, of items of theoretical knowledge, where there is no corresponding external object and where the memory is not an image but 'the thing itself'. How does the mind come to know such things and recognise them as true? Can it be that they are already present in some recess of the memory? In this case the work of thinking (cogito) is that of bringing out or shepherding ideas. This idea clearly owes much to the Platonic doctrine of *reminiscence* and, perhaps, also to the way it is formulated in the *Theaetetus.* Although Augustine in his *Retractions* explictly rejected his earlier acceptance of the doctrine, that was in the context of the pre-existence of the soul, which presented obvious difficulties to a Christian. It was possible for Augustine to retain that part of the theory which emphasised the transcendent origin of basic concepts (Platonic Forms) while rejecting the notion of the prior existence of the soul. Even for Plotinus the essence of the idea of a transcendent source for true knowledge is not the prior existence of the soul or mind but rather its priority in the sense of transcendence. The idea of transcendentally caused ideas can therefore be retained basically intact by Augustine.

To add to his sense of awe at the powers of memory Augustine now makes the further observation that we can sometimes remember the very act of recalling something, i.e. second order memory. But more important is the addition of a further three classes of memory items which are not dependent on external objects: numbers, dimensions and feelings. Our ability to count, he argues, does not derive from counting actual objects, but rather from the concept of number already present in our minds. It is, in other words, a prior condition of counting. Similarly diagrams made by architects express the idea in their mind. This is clearly another instance of Plato's example in the *Republic* of geometrical diagrams which express a principle rather than being the image of a specific physical object. The analysis of feelings leads him to make further stimulating distinctions and observations. To begin with he distinguishes the feeling I might have of pain from that of desire, fear, joy and sadness. The former is the recollection by the memory of a bodily sensation, that is the recollection of something external and therefore an image of it. But the emotions, while sometimes connected with external objects, are not in any sense images of them. Moreover I can have a memory of happiness when I am in a state of sadness, or the reverse. Thus the mind can reflect on its own condition. In an attempt to explain this self-reflection he adduces an analogy – that of the cow's stomach, in which a past meal is stored and can be regurgitated. But the analogy he finds to be unsatisfactory, since when we recall an emotion we do not experience it again, as we do with the food. For instance, we can recall fear without now being afraid.

Augustine finally adds the conundrum of how it is that we can remember forgetfulness apparently by means of memory. And by this he says he does not mean just the word itself but the very idea of forgetfulness (there is a difference between the word as sound and as concept).[28] He has now reached an impasse. But the importance of these chapters of the *Confessions* is what it reveals to us about Augustine as a philosopher. There is a determination to pursue an enquiry, the delight and stimulation of the problems posed, the range of subtle and useful distinctions that are made in the course of his analysis, and the self-criticism of his own analogies. We may then add to this what is particularly characteristic of Augustine, a philosophising which starts from the self and analyses the self and secondly the end point of this analysis which is never lost to sight, the search for the divine which is ultimately found within. It is at this crucial stage of his analysis that he pauses to reflect on the difficulty and the nature of his enquiry which is one of self-investigation:

> Who is to carry the research beyond this point? Who can understand the truth of the matter? O, Lord, I am working hard in this field, and the field of my labours is my own self. I have become a problem to myself, like land which a farmer works only with difficulty and at the cost of much sweat. For I am not now investigating the tracts of the heavens, or measuring the distance of the stars, or trying to discover how the earth hangs in space. I am investigating myself, my memory, my mind.[29]

Although Augustine's examination of perception and memory probably traces in some way the direction and development of his own philosophical researches, it is represented here in the *Confessions* as part of a tightly constructed argument which begins and ends with the search for god. Each of the distinctions made along the way finds its place in this ultimate search. For god is not to be identified with any of the things which sense-experience conveys to our memories, nor is he to be identified with theoretical knowledge, number, geometry or emotions. Although the emotion of joy may be close to that of happiness, the traditional aim of Greek philosophy, true happiness, is more than joy. But if we are to find god, we can only find him if we recognise him, and to this extent he is already present to our memory.

> You were within me, and I was in the world outside myself. I searched for you outside myself and, disfigured as I was, I fell upon the lovely things of your creation. You were with me, but I was not with you.[30]

But he is in no way confined and in this sense while found within us he is above our memory and to be reached only by striving beyond ourselves:

> You are always there above me, and as I rise up towards you in my mind, I shall go beyond even this force which is in me, this force which we call memory, longing to reach out to you by the only possible means and to cling to you in the only way in which it is possible to cling to you.[31]

This strong contrast and balance between finding god within and at the same time affirming his otherness and transcendence has much in common with the way in which the Neoplatonists stress the superiority of transcendent cognition (as opposed to cognition based on sense-perception) as the key to the discovery of the self and the divine while at the same time affirming the complete otherness and transcendence of the One, which can only be reached by transcending the intellect.

Mysticism

In several passages in the *Confessions* Augustine mentions what seem to be mystical experiences. The clearest and most interesting of these is his description of a prayerful moment enjoyed with his mother at Ostia not long before her death. There are many similarities with

Plotinus which may be due both to the borrowing of ideas to express his own thoughts and to the often common experiences of mystics within particular cultures. The context is one of prayerful discussion of the happiness of the saints. We note in particular the ordered ascent of the soul from level to level:

> As the flame of love burned stronger in us and raised us higher towards the eternal God, our thoughts ranged over the whole compass of material things in their various degrees, up to the heavens themselves, from which the sun and the moon and the stars shine down upon the earth. Higher still we climbed, thinking and speaking all the while in wonder at all that you have made. At length we came to our own souls and passed beyond them to that place of everlasting plenty, where you feed Israel for ever with the food of truth.[32]

As in Plotinus the context here is one of philosophical discussion. It begins with the physical world just as in Plotinus' interpretation of the *Symposium* as the ascent of the soul from physical to intellectual Beauty. From the exterior creation of the divine it moves with the soul to the interior self, then finally beyond soul to a level which is reminiscent of the Intelligible world of Plotinus, that is also a world of 'plenty', borrowing an image from the *Symposium*, since it contains the causes of all. This becomes even clearer in what follows in which the timeless (eternal) nature of the divine is emphasised:

> There life is that Wisdom by which all these things that we know are made, all things that ever have been and all that are yet to be. But that Wisdom is not made: it is as it has always been and as it will be for ever – or, rather, I should not say that it has been or will be, for it simply is, because eternity is not in the past or in the future. And while we spoke of the eternal Wisdom, longing for it and straining for it with all the strength of our hearts, for one fleeting instant we reached out and touched it. Then with a sigh, leaving our spiritual harvest bound to it, we returned to the sound of our own speech, in which each word has a beginning and an ending.

Much here is familiar from Plotinus – the description of eternity as an eternal present, the reaching out beyond to the divine, the momentary grasping of it, the metaphors of touching, and the resigned return to the time-world of discursive thought. Of course there are great differences too, primarily in the Christian content and expression, and the telescoping of Plotinus' One and Intellect. This notion of incorporeality was also one of the elements which helped to form his notion of divinity. Other influences at work here were Plotinus' One which contributed to the concept of a god who is simple, transcendent and ineffable.[33]

Evil

A dangerous tendency in Augustine's earlier thought was his equation of the physical world with evil. Plotinus' philosophy of Being and its identity with the Good helped him to overcome this. And so in the *Confessions* he argues that god as good is the source of being which must then be good. Further that where there is an absence of all good, Being too must be absent, i.e. there would not be anything. Only good, then, is substance and evil is not substance but the absence of being and of good.

> So we must conclude that if things are deprived of all good, they cease altogether to be; and this means that as long as they are, they are good. Therefore, whatever is, is good; and evil, the origin of which I was trying to find, is not a substance, because if it were a substance, it would be good.[34]

Epistemology

We have already referred to the active power of the soul in Augustine's theory of sense-perception in his work *On the Magnitude of the Soul*. This is seen both in the way in which the power of soul extends, as it were, beyond the confines of the physical body so that the act of sensation takes place at the point of the object, and also in the way in which the inner processing of sense data is an act of soul on the received impressions, something which is clearly seen in the context of inferences that are made about physical objects from other objects which are actually seen, e.g. that there is fire from the observation of smoke,[35] and in the case of our recalling perceptions of objects that are no longer present to us in their physical form.[36] Plotinus had made a similar observation in the context of memory.[37]

Time and eternity

Augustine's interest in the philosophy of time derives to a large extent from his speculations about god's creation of the universe. These were partly occasioned by his own personal rejection and escape from the doctrines of Manicheanism in which the created world is seen as an aberrant creation not willed by god himself. In this context there arose the inevitable connection between the created world characterised by time and god's eternal nature. The topic aroused in Augustine a deep philosophical curiosity as it had also done in Plotinus. He expresses in similar words the mental puzzle occasioned by the concept of time, which seems so simple at first sight but becomes fraught with problems as soon as we start to investigate more deeply and ask what time is. Like Plotinus, Augustine distinguishes both between time and eternity and between time and what is in time. It is difficult not to suppose some influence here. But in each case there are differences. As in Plotinus the concept of temporal priority is to be applied to the relationship between things in the physical world, even to the movement of the heavenly bodies. All of these things manifest time, but time is not to be identified with their movement. Time itself is an aspect of the soul. But whereas for Plotinus time as the life of the soul has a sort of existence in itself – in fact it is identified primarily with the life of the universal soul rather than that of the individual – for Augustine time is applicable to the individual soul and to the way in which it sees the events of the phenomenal world, past, present and future. One could say, then, that time is subjective. Augustine's great interest in memory is brought once more into play. To speak exactly, there is no past or future, for all is the present. The past is the present memory of things past, the present the present perception of things present and the future the present expectation of what will be.[38] His tentative conclusion is that time is an extension of the mind:

> It seems to me then that time is merely an extension, though of what it is an extension I do not know. I begin to wonder whether it is an extension of the mind itself.[39]

Time in fact comes into being only with the creation of the physical world. Time is a characteristic of the created world as opposed to the eternal life of the creator. This is quite different from Plotinus who stresses the role of Soul as time-life and therefore intermediary between the eternity of Intellect and the physical world as the manifestation of time. Moreover for Augustine the same distinction between creator and created holds between man, as created and time-bound, and god as eternal. This strong distinction makes it difficult to see how, if at all, man can escape entirely from being time-bound without confusing his nature with that of god which is characterised by eternity. The life of the saints is at most 'everlasting'.[40] But perhaps Augustine is just being more cautious in expression than other Christian mystics who came closer to declaring the identification of the mystic with the divine.

Contemplation and the ascent of the soul

At the end of his treatise *On the Magnitude of the Soul* Augustine enumerates seven stages by which the soul rises or returns to god. In effect they can be grouped into three and the influence of the Platonic tradition is evident. First are the stages which are concerned with the soul's relationship to the body and the physical world. There follow those concerned with the soul 'by itself' and finally the stages which lead to the encounter with God. In the particular context of this treatise the focal point is the soul's power, that is the magnitude of soul in terms of its incorporeal power rather than of physical size; thus at the lower level we recognise the power of the soul as giving life to the body and keeping it as a unity. The next stage takes us beyond the 'vegetative' powers to the powers of sensation and then beyond these to the powers that are peculiar to man, his rational powers. In all of this we are reminded of the method which Plotinus in V.1 exhorts us to follow in recognising the different levels of our own activities. The transition is then made to the transcendent powers of soul, its ability to separate itself from the flesh in an act of self-purification. The fifth stage is that of being in a state of purification and involves the positive movement towards god. The distinction between two levels of purification, a negative and a positive, suggest the influence of Porphyry who had formalised into two phases what is only implied in Plotinus. The sixth stage is characterised by the steady gaze of the eye of the soul on its goal. The ultimate goal is described as follows:

> What shall I say are the delights, what the enjoyment, of the supreme and true God; what breadth of undisturbed peace and eternity? These are the wonders that great souls have declared, so far as they brought themselves to speak of

these realities, great souls of incomparable greatness who, we believe, beheld and now behold these things.[41]

THE EASTERN TRADITION

As in the West, so also in the Eastern part of the Roman Empire, it was not only the Neoplatonists who influenced Christian thinkers. They owe much to the Stoics, to Aristotle and to the tradition of earlier Platonism. Platonism especially had always proved an attractive source of ideas as can be seen from earlier Christian thinkers such as Justin and Origen (184–255). All these philosophical strands had been absorbed in different ways and in differing degrees by Christian writers before Plotinus, but the thought of Plotinus and those Platonists influenced by him was the predominant vehicle of influence in Late Antiquity. Despite the problems presented by Neoplatonism to orthodox Christianity, these Christian writers could still draw on Plato. Christian teaching on the soul was in some ways closer to that of Aristotle with the stress on the close soul–body connection, but the ethos of spiritual escape was appealing and the Platonic teaching on the ascent of the soul profoundly influential with its stress on purification, contemplation and union with god. Perhaps the most interesting and important group of Christian theologians to be influenced in this way were the three Cappadocians, Basil (330–379), Gregory of Nazianzen (329–390) and Gregory of Nyssa (died 394), the brother of Basil. It is difficult to be certain whether or to what extent they were directly familiar with pagan Neoplatonic writings. It is likely that Basil had at least come in contact with two fundamental treatises of Plotinus, V.1 which gives the outline of his system and VI.9 on the One. Although Gregory of Nyssa may have had his knowledge of Plotinus from his brother, it is more likely that he had direct access to some of the *Enneads.* What is, however, more important for us is the emergence of some of the same philosophical themes and similar solutions in Basil, Gregory of Nyssa and Plotinus. In the case of Gregory of Nazianzen we know that he had studied philosophy in Athens, for he openly acknowledged his debt to his Platonic teachers.[42] Like Synesius, these Christian Platonists were much concerned with the origin of the universe, but defended the orthodox doctrine that the world is not eternal while at the same time owing a great deal to the Platonic view of the relationship of god to the physical universe as suggested in the *Timaeus.* The creator could be compared with Plato's demiurge. They were also deeply influenced by the notion of negative theology as espoused by Plotinus, by the Neoplatonic schemas of a universal hierarchy and the descent and return of the human soul.

Origin of the universe

We have already referred to Basil's accepting the logic of the argument for the eternity of the universe with his insistance that creation in time was a matter of revelation. He nevertheless still finds a difficulty in the concept of a first moment of time. Maximus Confessor (580–662) has a more radical solution which envisages the transformation and glorification of the whole universe:

> When the generation of men has reached its completion, with its end time also comes to a stop, and so the restoration of the universe happens, and, with the change of the whole, humanity is changed, from the corruptible and earthy to the impassible and everlasting.[43]

This is another way of asserting the eternity of the universe, though in a transformed state.

Hierarchy

The Cappadocian Fathers divided reality into three realms, that of the physical world, that of the angels which they termed the intelligible world and which was divided from the physical world by the firmament of the heavens. The physical world is a shadow or copy of the intelligible. Above this again was God. Man was unique in belonging to both the intelligible and physical worlds. His origin is in the intelligible but he descends to the physical. His destiny is to return again to the intelligible. Both his descent and return occur in three stages. From his origin in the intelligible he descends to the physical world but can descend even further into sin. This is very similar to Plotinus' observation, especially in IV.8, that man is destined to become embodied and serve the universe, but can avoid a deeper and more involved descent into matter. It is an idea expressed by Synesius, and others, as the difference between service as a servant and as a slave.[44] The return of the soul is similarly influenced by the Neoplatonic ascent of the soul, but expressed in a framework borrowed from the experience of St Paul. The first stage is that of purification which brings the soul to the level of the firmament, the first heaven of St Paul. This is followed by illumination or the acquisition of wisdom which brings the soul to the intelligible level or second heaven. There remains the final stage of ascent to the third heaven, variously described as deification or union with God. In some ways one could say that Gregory of Nyssa's work *On the Creation of Man*, which deals with the descent and return of the soul, is a Christian version of the Neoplatonic descent/ascent of the soul. The theme of purification and the return of the soul is also dealt with by Gregory of Nyssa in his treatise *On Virginity.* The following passage, which is worth quoting in full, displays a close affinity with the *Symposium* and the spirit of Plotinus' interpretation in I.6, *On Beauty.* Particularly noteworthy is the positive evaluation of physical beauty as an aid or stepping-stone to intelligible beauty, a balance, as so often in Plotinus, to the negative and ascetic attitude to the physical:

> Accordingly, in the search for the beautiful, the person who is superficial in his thought when he sees something in which fantasy is mixed with some beauty, will think that the thing itself is beautiful because of its own nature, his attention being attracted to it because of pleasure and he will be concerned with nothing beyond this. But the man who has purified the eye of his soul is able to look at such things and forget the matter in which the beauty is encased and he uses what he sees as a kind of basis for his contemplation of intelligible beauty. By participation in this beauty the other beautiful things come into being and are identified.[45]

Another Plotinian idea which Gregory of Nyssa develops is that of negative theology or *aphairesis*, which is important, as it was for Plotinus, not only for his concept of god but equally so for the way in which the soul ascends to the divine by purification, i.e. the stripping away of all impediments, both conceptual and moral, in our attempt to reach out to him. Thus the metaphysical principle is at the same time a principle of spiritual action.

The influence of Neoplatonic triads also appears, particularly in Gregory of Nazianzen, who analyses god into Father, son and spirit, and Beginning, middle and end. This is seen more precisely in the triad, Monad, Dyad, Triad, as applied to the Christian Trinity and the obviously Neoplatonic triad Rest, procession, return, applied to vertical relationships in the hierarchy of being in order to explain the procession of reality from higher powers.

In conclusion we may refer to two Christian thinkers, Dionysius and Boethius, from East and West respectively, who had a profound influence in the formation of medieval thought by their transmission of Neoplatonic ideas.

Dionysius

It is strange that the close liaison of certain kinds of Neoplatonism with religion, though provoking fierce criticism and scorn from Christian thinkers, provided, in the curious 'cover' of Dionysius the Areopagite, a basis for sacramental theology. We do not know the real identity of this writer, who purported to be the member of the Areopagus Council converted by St Paul. The disguise may have been intended either to gain prestige for his publications or, perhaps, to avoid possible condemnation for heresy and a too obviously close affinity to pagan Neoplatonism. For this writer, by taking up the theurgical theories of Proclus, effectively transposed the ideas first adumbrated by Iamblichus into a Christian ritual context. But more important was his adaptation of the complex structure of Proclus' transcendent world to the needs of Christianity. In particular he exploited the triadic and monadic structure of each level. The most basic triads were those of rest, procession and return (*mone, proodos, epistrophe*), unparticipated, participated, participating (*amethektos, methektos, metechon*), and being, power and activity (*ousia, dunamis, energeia*). Our approach to reality is made through three theological levels, the Symbolic, Cataphatic and Mystical, which guide us through the hierarchical structure of the universe from the physical world to God himself. Each of these levels represents a stage in the ascent of the soul to God. The Symbolic theology fosters our purification; the Cataphatic, which is the equivalent of the Intelligible universe in which positive affirmations are made of the divine, is the level of illumination; and finally the Mystical leads the soul to union (*henosis*) with God as the One. The articulations (*diacosmeseis*) within and between these different levels describe the entities that make up the structure or hierarchies through which the soul must travel in its journey to God. For example at the level of Symbolic theology the levels may be divided into the Legal, Ecclesiastical and Celestial hierarchies: the Legal represents things in the world, the Ecclesiastical the people and the Celestial the angels. At each level we must also distinguish Mysteries, Initiator and

Initiate. At the Ecclesiastical level, for example, the Mysteries are the scriptures and the sacraments, the initiators the priests, and the initiates the faithful. Each of these in turn appears at different levels: the Eucharist above the other sacraments, the bishop beyond the priest, the confirmed Christian above the Catechumen. And so we are presented with an elaborate structure which both explains the metaphysical structure of reality and acts as the framework within which the spiritual progress of the individual can be fostered.

Our ascent takes us from the expression of the divine in this world to the archetypes at the intelligible level of the Cataphatic theology. Here the triads are more united, just as Intellect and its object are one, and each level implies the others. But the soul must pass beyond this level of knowledge:

> Unto this darkness which is beyond light we pray that we may come, and may attain to vision through the loss of sight and knowledge, and that in ceasing thus to see or to know we may learn to know that which is beyond all perception and understanding (for this emptying of our faculties is true sight and knowledge), and that we may offer him that transcends all things the praises of a transcendent hymnody, which we shall do by denying or removing all things that are – like as men who, carving a statue out of marble, remove all the impediments that hinder the clear perception of the latent image and by this mere removal display the hidden statue itself in its hidden beauty.[46]

The transcendent hymn, the step beyond knowledge, the stripping away of everything and the creation of the beautiful statue, all remind us of the long tradition of the soul's ascent in Platonic philosophy. And just as in Plotinus so here too the final step in negative theology reveals the positive. Dionysius, however, is that much more boldy positive in his designation of God as *hyperousios*, a super-being who transcends both being and non-being.

Boethius

It is appropriate to conclude with Boethius not only because of the influence of his best-known work, *The Consolation of Philosophy,* throughout the Middle Ages but because of the undoubted Neoplatonic influence found in that work. Boethius was certainly familiar with the work of Porphyry whose *Introduction* to the logic of

Aristotle he translated, but it is now becoming clearer that he also had access to the later Platonists working in the Eastern part of the empire, probably through the work of Proclus, though it still remains doubtful whether he ever travelled to Athens or even to Alexandria as some scholars have suggested.

The goodness of the universe

The main source of consolation which Boethius found in philosophy during his imprisonment for treason was the essential freedom of the human soul from its mortal body. The main theme of the *Consolation* is thus the Platonic one of leading the soul back from alienation to its real home. Platonic, too, is the optimistic note struck when he praises the harmony and beauty of the universe in the poem at 3.9. It is based clearly on the *Timaeus* but as seen through Neoplatonic eyes:

> All things Thou bringest forth from Thy high archetype:
> Thou, height of beauty, in Thy mind the beauteous world
> Dost bear, and in that ideal likeness shaping it,
> Dost order perfect parts a perfect whole to frame ...
> From causes like Thou bringest forth souls and lesser lives,
> Which from above in chariots swift Thou dost disperse
> Through sky and earth, and by Thy law benign they turn
> And back to Thee they come through fire that brings them home.

In this celebration of the earth as the beautiful product of the divine we note a number of ideas which are later elaborations of Plato, e.g. the notion that the model of the earth is in God's mind, the descent of souls on 'chariots' echoing the developed Neoplatonic theory of soul vehicles, and not least the concept of 'return'. These are just a few instances in this short poem which betrays many other examples of Neoplatonic influence, some of which can be traced more particularly to Proclus.

Eternity

We have seen the importance to Plotinus of the concept of eternity as an essential characteristic of the intelligible world. Intellect in turn bestows eternity in a partial way on its product, the physical world; for, though in time, our world shares something of eternity in having no beginning or end. For Boethius, too, eternity was a key concept which influenced not only his view of the universe and its relationship to god but also the destiny of man himself. There remains some doubt as to whether Boethius, at least in the *Consolation,* accepted the eternity of the universe or whether the views of Plato and Aristotle that he reports were no more than reports. His main concern is to give a clear account of the eternity of the divine as different from the 'eternity' that might be applied to the physical universe. Eternity is non-durational and is applied to a life which is complete and all-together:

> Eternity therefore is the whole and perfect possession all together of a life which cannot end, which becomes clearer from a comparison with temporal things. For whatever lives in time progresses as something present from what is past to what is future, and there is nothing placed in time which could embrace the whole extent of its life equally.[47]

Although Boethius finds it difficult not to use language of eternity that might suggest duration of some kind ('remaining' 'cannot end' and 'always') it is quite clear from the contrast with the 'eternity' of the physical universe that he means eternity to be without duration:

> For it is one thing to be drawn through an endless life, which is what Plato attributed to the world, and another to have embraced equally the whole presence of a life that cannot end, which is clearly the special characteristic of the divine mind.

The distinction is finally marked in a clear manner by the application of two different names:

> Thus if we want to apply names appropriate to the things, let us say, following Plato, that God indeed is eternal (*aeternus*), but the world is perpetual (*perpetuus*).[48]

These are the formulations that provided Western theologians with a standard doctrine of divine eternity which Boethius had taken ultimately from Plotinus. It is the careful application of two distinct terms that is new in Boethius.[49] His clear concept of eternity also allowed him to make the important distinction, found already in Plotinus, between the lower world governed by Fate and the transcendent world characterised by divine providence. It is only in the transcendent world that true freedom can be attained. Moreover Fate is subordinate and subsumed under providence. In the lower world men regard providence as a seeing in advance of what is to come and acknowledge that this is only possible if there is a fixed or fated order. But in the transcendent world knowledge (god's knowledge) of 'what is to come' is simultaneous with its enactment, since it is a timeless realm. We must then rethink our notion of what divine providence is. And it is only when we ourselves reach this level that we find true freedom:

> His knowledge transcends all temporal change and abides in the immediacy of his presence. It embraces all the infinite recesses of past and future and views them in the immediacy of its knowing as though they are happening in the present. If you wish to consider, then, the foreknowledge or prevision by which he discovers all things, it will be more correct to think of it not as a kind of foreknowledge of the future, but as the knowledge of a never ending presence. So that it is better called providence or 'looking forth' than prevision or 'seeing beforehand'.[50]

Boethius was finally executed by the Gothic king Theoderic and so never completed his grand scheme to translate all of Aristotle and Plato into Latin. In fact he never got beyond translating and commenting on the *Categories* and *On Interpretation*, thus leaving the impression that he was mainly an Aristotelian. But this was no truer of him than of Simplicius, for the intention behind his project was to show the harmony of Aristotle and Plato. It is an appropriate point with which to conclude this introduction to the philosophy of Late Antiquity; for it has been centred, as I explained at the beginning, on Neoplatonism as the main vehicle of philosophical thought in Late Antiquity. Even the apparently independent pursuit of Aristotelian studies in this period was largely subsumed in the grand scheme of elaborating a perennial philosophy whose founding genius was Plato.

Conclusion

I have chosen in this chapter to illustrate the influence on Christian thinkers of the pagan philosophers of Late Antiquity by a selection of particular themes. In the final analysis, however, their greatest legacy was the systematic metaphysical structure which they devised, with its primary distinction of two distinct but interpenetrating worlds, the physical world of time and the transcendent world of eternity. Along with this they furnished the concepts to explore and delineate the complexities of transcendent reality. Happily, their ideas and the mental armoury which they supplied suited the increasing demands of a Christian intelligentsia for the means to express in discursive terms the truths of their religion. And yet while the ideas of the Neoplatonists continued throughout the Middle Ages and Renaissance to be the main vehicle of Platonism within a Christian world, they also deeply influenced the Islamic world. Moreover they have been and continue to be a rich source for metaphysical speculation that is not specifically linked to religious views. And so as one possible and rich interpretation of Plato's views Neoplatonism remains as universal as Plato himself.

NOTES

INTRODUCTION

1 Porphyry, *Life of Plotinus* chapter 14.
2 *Life of Plotinus* chapter 14.
3 Plotinus, *Enneads* V.1.
4 *Enneads* V.1.1,1f.
5 I.1.1,1f.

1 THE INDIVIDUAL

1 Plato, *Republic* IX 589A; Plotinus, *Enneads* V.l.10; I.1.10,15.
2 *Enneads* I.1.7.
3 I.1.7,13–14.
4 V.1.4,16–20.
5 IV.3.30,9.
6 See chapter 4, pp.53–55.
7 *Enneads* V.3.3,6–9.
8 V.1.11,1–7.
9 V.9.4,3–7.
10 V.1.12,19–21.
11 I.1.13,5–8.
12 V.3.4,7–12.
13 I.4.13.
14 I.4.8,4–6.
15 Aristotle, *de anima* 430a4–5.
16 Aristotle, *Metaphysics* 1075a4.
17 Cf. A. J. Ayer, *The Problem of Knowledge* (London 1956), pp.84–85: 'The problem of perception as the sceptic poses it, is that of justifying our belief in the existence of the physical objects which it is commonly taken for granted that we perceive ... What, according to them, is *immediately* given in perception is an evanescent object called an idea, or an impression, or a presentation, or a sense-datum, which is not only private to a single

observer but private to a single sense.' Bertrand Russell, *The Problems of Philosophy* (Oxford 1980), p.11: 'The real table, if there is one, is not immediately known to us at all but must be an inference from what is immediately known.'

18 *Enneads* V.5.1,18f.

19 V.5.1,50–55.

20 V.3.

21 V.1.10,5–8.

2 THE ONE

1 See chapter 7, p.95f.

2 Plotinus, *Enneads* VI.9.1.

3 V.6.3,2–4.

4 V.6.3,5–8.

5 See chapter 5, p.68ff.

6 VI.7.36,7–9 'We are taught about it by comparisons and negations and knowledge of the things which come from it.'

7 Aristotle, *Physics* 201a27–34; *Metaphysics* 1049b23–26; *de Generatione Animalium* 734a30–32. Appeal could also be made to the idea expressed in Plato (e.g. *Timaeus* 29e) that god does not begrudge the bestowal of his gifts; see *Enneads* IV.8.6,13f. 'all the power which was in those higher beings, ... could not stand still as if it had drawn a line round itself in selfish *jealousy*'; V.4.1, 34–36 'how then could the most perfect, the first Good, remain in itself as if it *grudged* to give of itself or was impotent, when it is the productive power of all things?'.

8 *Enneads* V.1.6,38–40.

9 VI.7.17,4–10.

10 V.3.15,37–40.

11 V.3.15,27–32.

12 V.2.1,3.

13 VI.9.6,52–55.

14 VI.7.31,1ff. 'But he is not even the "is"; for he has no need whatever even of this; for "he is good" is not applicable to him either, but to that to which the "is" applies.'

15 III.8.10,5–12.

16 Plato, *Timaeus* 42e5–6.

17 Plotinus, *Enneads* V.4.2,27–38.

18 Aristotle, *Metaphysics* 1072b3.

19 Plotinus, *Enneads* V.1.6,19f.

20 V.2.1.

3 INTELLECT

1 E.g. Xenophanes, Anaxagoras, Aristotle, the Stoics.

2 See Plotinus, *Enneads* V.1.7,4 borrowing an image from Plato, *Republic* VI 509b9–10. See also *Enneads* V.3.12,41.
3 For all of this see *Enneads* V.9.3.
4 V.9.9,7.
5 E.g. see *Enneads* V.9.3,22–24 'one intellect being like the shape on the bronze, and the other like the man who makes the shape in the bronze'.
6 See chapter 1, p.10.
7 Plato, *Timaeus* 28cf.
8 *Enneads* V.9.6,11f.
9 V.9.8,3f.
10 Further on the unity in plurality of Intellect VI.7.17,24f.
11 II.5.3.
12 For the latter see the discussion of VI.7 on p. 35 where a horse, though non-rational in this world, is potentially intellectual in that its archetype was in the intelligible.
13 VI.2.20,19ff.
14 V.9.6,3.
15 See chapter 1, p.14f.
16 Aristotle, *Metaphysics* 1074b34.
17 Plotinus, *Enneads* V.9.5,15.
18 V.9.7,13f. 'that which is thought of is prior to thinking'.
19 V.9.8,8f.
20 V.3.5.
21 V.3.5,42–43.
22 See, for example, the discussion of Victorinus in chapter 8.
23 Aristotle, *Metaphysics* 11.6, 1071b12ff.
24 Plotinus, *Enneads* V.3.5,33f.
25 *Enneads* V.5.1,40f.
26 Plato, *Sophist* 254bff.
27 Plotinus, *Enneads* VI.7.12,23.
28 VI.7.9.
29 VI.7.9,11 'For here perhaps man is rational, but in that world there is the man before reasoning.'
30 V.2.2,26–30.
31 For the equivalence of activity and life see VI.7.17,10f where referring to the One as transcending actuality (Intellect) he says 'so if there is anything prior to actuality, it transcends actuality, so that it also transcends life'.
32 See chapter 1, pp.9–10 and *Enneads* V.2.1.
33 Cf. V.1.7,15f 'Intellect, certainly, by its own means even defines its being for itself by the power which comes to it from the One.'
34 V.1.7,25–27.
35 VI.7.17,17f. 'and the form was in that which was shaped but the shaper was shapeless'.
36 III.8.32f.

37 VI.9.5,29.
38 See, for example, the Gnostic Valentinus cited by Irenaeus, *adv. Haer.* I.2.2ff.
39 V.3.11,4–9.
40 V.5.7.
41 The distinction of light and objects illuminated is a clear reference to the key passage of Plato's *Republic* with the analogy of the sun (Plato, *Republic* 507eff.).
42 Plato, *Symposium* 203b5.
43 VI.7.35,20–28.
44 VI.2.22,26f.
45 III.8.7.16–17.

4 SOUL, THE UNIVERSE AND MATTER

1 Plotinus, *Enneads* IV.8.4,32.
2 Porphyry, *Life of Plotinus* 13.
3 Plotinus, *Enneads* IV. 3 and 4.
4 For Thales see Aristotle, *de anima* 411a8 'Thales thought that everything was full of gods'; Plato, *Timaeus* 36d; for the Stoics see Cicero, *On the Nature of the Gods* II.29f.
5 Aristotle, *Physics* 199b28–29.
6 Plotinus, *Enneads* III.8.4,22–28.
7 III.8.8,14–17.
8 III.8.4,8–11.
9 II.1.5, 9ff.
10 VI.4.15,9–14.
11 See p.56f. below.
12 *Enneads* IV.3.9,39–41.
13 IV.3.20.
14 VI.5.6.
15 The term *logos* (word) points to something as being an expression or manifestation, as the physical word is the external expression of the idea in the mind or a definition is the 'expression' of an object. Although the term has a long history Plotinus makes particular use of the Stoic concept of 'seminal logoi'.
16 *Enneads* IV.3.22,1–7.
17 VI.4.7,23ff.
18 IV.5.6–7.
19 *Republic* 507–509.
20 *Enneads* V.5.7.
21 IV.3.21.
22 E.g. Herophilus of Chalcedon and Erasistratus of Ceos (third century BC) identified the brain as the centre of the nervous system and the location of the mind. Their findings were accepted by the Platonic physician Galen (second century AD). Plato located the

mind in the head (*Timaeus* 44d–e) whereas Aristotle (and Alexander of Aphrodisias), the Stoics and the Epicureans placed it in the heart.

23 *Enneads* IV.3.23.
24 VI.4.7.
25 VI.4.7,4–18.
26 Aristotle, *de anima* 411b5–14.
27 *Enneads* IV.3.10,31f.
28 VI.7.4 and 5.
29 VI.7.5,30.
30 Plato, *Parm.* 131c1–3. In his commentary on this passage Proclus (*in Parm.* 864–865) says that Plato is holding up for our instruction a certain stage in the development towards a full philosophical approach that is characterised by the use of 'imagination'. This faculty prevents us from seeing true incorporeality and thus it is appropriate at this point in the dialogue to employ an analogy implying division in the Forms themselves.
31 Aristotle, *Metaphysics* 991a20f.
32 *Physics* 267b6–9. See also H. Cherniss, *Aristotle's Criticism of Plato and the Academy* (New York 1944), p.371.
33 Plotinus, *Enneads* V.9.1,7f.
34 IV.6.2,5–7.
35 IV.6.2,18–19.
36 VI.2.22.29–32.
37 VI.4.4,39.
38 V.1.1,3f.
39 III.7.11,14.
40 IV.8.
41 IV.8.1,1–12.
42 IV.8.1,42–44.
43 IV.3.14 end.
44 IV.3.13,17–21.
45 IV.8.7,26f.
46 IV.4.8, especially 34ff.
47 IV.4.8,14f. 'And when the soul's activity is directed to other things, and completely directed to them, it will not accept the memory of things like these when they have passed away, since it is not aware of the sense-impression produced by them when they are there.'
48 II.9.18,30ff; IV.3.18.
49 III.7.
50 Cf. Plato, *Timaeus* 37d3 'the nature of the living being is eternal'.
51 *Enneads* III.7.2,17–19.
52 III.7.4,3–5.
53 III.7.6,22–27.
54 I.5 [*On whether well-being increases with time*].7,22–26.
55 See above, chapter 1 p. 13f.
56 *Enneads* III.7.11,29–34.

57 IV.4.1,29–31.
58 The 'receptacle' of *Timaeus* 49a–b and the 'disorderly motion' of *Timaeus* 30a.
59 Plato, *Timaeus* 48e–52d.
60 Plotinus, *Enneads* II.4.10,8.
61 I.8.10.
62 Aristotle, *Physics* I.7–9.
63 Plotinus, *Enneads* III.6.11,20f.
64 II.4.5,12.
65 IV.3.9,23–26.
66 III.6.11–14.
67 For the soul as creator of matter see III.9.3,7–16 and III.4.1.
68 III.9.3,15f.
69 See the report in Aristotle, *Metaphysics* A 6. 987b18ff.
70 See *Enneads* II.9.2,9–10.
71 Plutarch, *On Isis and Osiris* 369E. Numenius Fr. 52D with his idea of two souls. On this see Dillon, *The Middle Platonists* pp.203f. and 373f.
72 See, above all, *Enneads* II.9.
73 III.2.7,15ff.

5 THE RETURN OF THE SOUL

1 Plotinus, *Enneads* V.1.12 end.
2 Plato, *Theaetetus* 176a–b.
3 *Enneads* I.2.6,8ff.
4 Plato, *Phaedo* 69b–c.
5 *Enneads* V.1.1.
6 I.2.5 end.
7 In his *Letter to Marcella* 4 Porphyry explains to his newly wedded wife that he is absent from home 'for the needs of the Hellenes'. This cryptic phrase, which appears to suggest a pagan Greek agenda, may refer to preparatory discussions to the great persecution of Diocletian and Galerius. It is possible also that his work *Against the Christians* had a practical purpose. For Iamblichus' link with matters of practical politics see Dominic O'Meara, 'A Neoplatonist ethics for high-level officials: Sopatros' Letter to Himerios', in *Philosophy and Society in Late Antiquity*. Proclus was so involved in protecting pagan interests through the local council at Athens that he had to go into exile for a short period (see Marinus, *Life of Proclus* 15).
8 For example the eleventh century writer Miskswayh draws on Porphyry's commentary on Aristotle's *Ethics* in his *Tahdib al-Akhlaq* (*Refinement of Character*) and Al-Amiri (tenth century), who also used Porphyry's commentary, places texts of Plato and Aristotle side by side for comparison, probably drawing on a Greek author

(Porpyhry?) who had done the same in order to show the compatibility of the two philosophers.

9 *Enneads* III.8.4,40–45.

10 See chapter 1, p.13f.

11 Chapter 8.

12 See chapter 1, p.10ff.

13 See Richard Wallis, 'Nous as Experience', pp.121–151 in *Neoplatonism and Indian Thought*, ed. R. Baine Harris (Norfolk, Virginia 1973).

14 E.g. Jan Van Ruusbroec, the thirteenth-century Flemish theologian and mystic, who teaches that the soul should both be active (in works of charity) and rest in God at the same time: 'God's Spirit drives us towards loving and virtuous activity, and he draws us back in to rest and enjoy. Therefore, to go in in idle enjoyment and to go out in virtuous activity and to remain constantly united with God's Spirit, this is what I mean.' *Werken* III, Van VII Trappen, ed. L. Reypens (Tielt: Lannoo, 1947), p.269.

15 *Enneads* IV.8.8,1–4.

16 Cf. Proclus, *in Tim.* III.333,29f.; Ps.-Simplicius, *in de anima* 6,12–17. Cf. H. J. Blumenthal, 'The Psychology of Plotinus and Later Platonism', p.273f. in *The Perennial Tradition of Neoplatonism*, ed. J. Cleary (Leuven 1997).

17 *Enneads* V.5.12,7–9.

18 I.6.7,1–6.

19 I.6.9,8–15 'Go back into yourself and look; and if you do not yet see yourself beautiful, then, just as someone making a statue which has to be beautiful cuts away here and polishes there and makes one part smooth and clears another till he has given his statue a beautiful face, so you too must cut away excess and straighten the crooked and clear the dark and make it bright and never stop "working on your statue" (cf. Plato, *Phaedrus* 252d7) till the divine glory of virtue shines out on you.' For Glaucus see Plato, *Republic* X, 611C.

20 *Enneads* VI.8.21,26–28.

21 III.4.3,21–23.

22 V.3.7.

23 VI.7.36,9–10.

24 V.1.6,5ff.

25 V.1.2. Compare this with the Christian Platonist Synesius who expresses a similar idea in the formal context of a philosophical hymn, I.72–94 'Let the aether and air be silent; let the sea be still.'

26 Plotinus, *Enneads* V.5.5,3–5; Plato, *Letter* VII 341c/d.

27 *Enneads* VI.7.22.

28 V.1.11,7–15.

29 VI.9.8,19–21.

30 VI.9.11.

Part II
6 PHILOSOPHY AND RELIGION

1 Porphyry, *Life of Plotinus* chapter 10.
2 Plotinus, *Enneads* IV.4.42,10f.
3 *Enneads* VI.7.14,20f.
4 IV.4.42,13–16.
5 IV.4.12.
6 II.3.7,12.
7 The Greek text of the fragments may be found in Smith, *Porphyrii Fragmenta*, pp.407–435. Most of them come from Eusebius' *Praeparatio evangelica* of which translations are available.
8 *Porphyrii Fragmenta*, 303F from Eusebius, *Praeparatio evangelica* IV.6,2f.
9 *Theurgy*, composed from the word *theos* (god) and *ergon* (work, act), is itself ambiguous and can mean 'act of the gods' or 'act on the gods'.
10 These ideas are found in Augustine, *City of God*, and Augustine is reporting from a book, treatise or section of a larger work, which he calls *On the Return of the Soul* (*de regressu animae*). Of course Augustine has his own agenda, part of which is to show that Porphyry failed to find such a way of salvation because it is found only in Christianity.
11 The Greek *pneumatikos* is the equivalent of the Latin *spiritalis*.
12 See the story from Porphyry recounted by Augustine, *City of God* X.9.45f. 'A good Chaldaean "astrologer" complained that his energetic efforts to purify a soul have been frustrated, because a powerful practitioner of the same art had been led by envy to conjure the powers with sacred spells and had bound them, to prevent their granting his requests'.
13 Porphyry cited by Eusebius, *Praeparatio evangelica* V.10,11f. 'Wisdom is cultivated in vain by those who devise for themselves intercourse with the higher power if they omit this aspect (happiness) from their considerations while bothering the divine mind about finding a runaway slave, the purchase of property, whether there will be a marriage, or a commercial transaction.'
14 Porphyry, *On Abstinence* II.24.1.
15 *On Abstinence* II.61.1. Although this is in fact a citation from Theophrastus, it is so totally integrated into Porphyry's own text as to express his own sentiments.
16 Plato, *Laws* 716d.
17 Porphyry, *On Abstinence* II.28.2.
18 *On Abstinence* II.36.22f.
19 Porphyry, *Philosophy from Oracles* in Augustine, *City of God* XIX.23.
20 Porphyry, *To Marcella* 16, p.284,24–25.
21 *To Marcella* 86, p.286,3–4.

22 *To Marcella* 18, p.286,6–8.
23 *To Marcella* 19.
24 Plato, *Laws* 905d,908e.
25 Porphyry in Iamblichus *de mysteriis* 145,4–7; 147,16–148,2; 150,3–5.
26 *myst.* 123,12–124,6.
27 *myst.* 124,5–6.
28 *myst.* III.28–30.
29 *myst.* II.11.
30 Plato, *Phaedo* 99a; Aristotle, *de anima* 416a14; for the Stoics see Cicero, *On Fate* 40–43.
31 Cf. Simplicius, *in Cat.* 2.13f; 116.25f.
32 For example, he does not consider it necessary to prove how evil can occur, if we can demonstrate that god cannot be its source; cf. *myst.* IV.6.
33 Plutarch 408D.
34 Damascius, *Commentary on the Phaedo* 123,3f.
35 Eunapius, *Lives of the Sophists* VI.1.5.
36 See his praise of Iamblichus in *Hymn to King Helios* 146A.
37 *Hymn to King Helios* 132C.
38 *Hymn to King Helios* 130C–D.
39 See chapter 1, p.12. Cf. Plotinus, *Enneads* V.3.4,11.
40 Plotinus, *Enneads* II.4.3,22.
41 See below, chapter 7, pp.100–103.
42 Cf. Proclus, *Elements of Theology* 57,59,140.
43 This is a short passage of Proclus with the heading 'on the hieratic art', found and published by J. Bidez (*Catalogue des manuscrits alchimiques grecs*, VI (Appendix O), pp.139–151, Brussels 1928). It is probably the original of Ficino's Latin translation of a piece of Proclus, *Opus Procli de sacrificio et magia* and the manuscript may have been the very one used by him.
44 Chapter ii. The Greek text with French translation may be found as an appendix in *Oracles Chaldaiques*, ed. E. Des Places (Paris 1971), p.207,17f.
45 *On the Chaldaean Philosophy* iv, p.210,29f. in the Des Places edition.
46 Sallustius, *On the Gods*. See the edition of A. D. Nock with introduction (Cambridge 1926).
47 On this see Robert Lamberton, *Homer the Theologian* (Berkeley 1986).

7 THE DEVELOPMENT OF NEOPLATONISM

1 Proclus, *Platonic Theology* I.1.
2 See Christoph Horn, *Plotin über Sein, Zahl und Einheit*, Teubner (Stuttgart/Leipzig 1995).
3 Porphyry, *Sententiae* 4.

4 *Sententiae* 37, p.33.3.
5 The Stoics believed that all that exists is corporeal. Thus god or the divine *pneuma* which is all present, is precisely that; it intermingles totally with the matter of the universe (see *Stoicorum Veterum Fragmenta* ii 310). The notion that two solids can occupy the same space is no longer anathema to modern physics, but was ridiculed in antiquity. Nevertheless the idea was borrowed by Porphyry and transformed to refer to the presence of the incorporeal (in fact even Stoic *pneuma* was hardly matter in the grossest sense), which like the Stoic divine substance was present everywhere but without changing its nature. Plotinus too made extensive use of Stoic ideas which he transformed to a higher metaphysical level.
6 Plotinus, *Enneads* III.4.6,27ff.
7 Porphyry, *Sententiae* 29.
8 *Sententiae* 18.
9 *Sententiae* 27.
10 *Sententiae* 34,35,40.
11 *Sententiae* 8.
12 See, for example, *Enneads* V.8.4,7–12.
13 Proclus, *The Elements of Theology*, Proposition 103.
14 See above chapter 2, pp.25–26.
15 Most notably Pierre Hadot in his *Porphyre et Victorine* (Paris 1968). See Smith, *Aufstieg und Niedergang des römischen Welt* (*ANRW*) II.36.2, pp.740–741 for some doubts.
16 See the report in Damascius *Princ.* I. 86,3ff.
17 *In Parm.* I.713,16–20. *Platonic Theology* II.10, p.63,18–20.
18 1072,19f.
19 1075,19–24.
20 1094,29f.
21 See chapter 3, p.32f.
22 See chapter 3, p.33f.
23 Some scholars think that Iamblichus had already developed the concept of *henads*.
24 Proclus, *The Elements of Theology* 21.
25 See chapter 3, p.35.
26 Plotinus, *Enneads* VI.7.9.
27 IV.7.
28 VI.4 and 5.
29 See chapter 4, p56f. on matter.
30 'That every cause operates both prior to its consequent and in conjunction with it, and likewise gives rise to further effects posterior to it.'
31 Proclus, *The Elements of Theology* Prop.57.
32 Aristotle, *Metaphysics* 990a13, Syrianus, *in met.* 110.18f.
33 Aquinas, *Summa contra Gentiles* III.74.
34 See chapter 6, pp.87–88.

35 Plato, *Republic* 379–380.
36 Proclus, *The Elements of Theology* Prop.204.

8 CHRISTIANITY AND NEOPLATONISM

1 Letter 105. Synesius' letters are one of the most personal and historically valuable sets of letters to survive from Late Antiquity and give a good idea of his engaging character as well as of the life of the times.
2 Sallustius, *On the Gods and the World* XX.
3 In a work specifically aimed against the Christians, *On the Eternity of the Universe against the Christians*, which is now lost and whose eighteen arguments can be reconstructed from the counter-work of Philoponus.
4 *Against Proclus on the Eternity of the Worl*d, translation by C. Wildberg (London and Ithaca, N.Y. 1987).
5 It is not altogether clear whether Justinian specifically aimed his legislation against the Academy or more generally against pagan educational institutions which taught law and rhetoric.
6 The only surviving work of Ammonius (his dates are uncertain: born 435–445, died 517–526) is his *Commentary on the 'de interpretatione' of Aristotle*. But his ideas are also incorporated as 'lecture notes' in the works of Asclepius and Philoponus. Ammonius had been a pupil of Proclus and became established in Alexandria in 485.
7 It used to be maintained that the Platonic school in Alexandria was not as much influenced by Neoplatonic ideas and retained the tradition of Middle-Platonism. The notion of a separate Alexandrian School of this kind has now been refuted by Ilsetraut Hadot, *Le Problème du Néoplatonisme Alexandrin: Hierocles et Simplicius* (Paris 1978), who has shown that the Alexandrians were in close touch with what was happening in Athens (there were frequent 'exchanges') and accepted the main tenets of Neoplatonism.
8 See Sorabji, 'Divine names and sordid deals in Ammonius' Alexandria', pp. 203–213 in *Philosophy and Society in Late Antiquity*, forthcoming 2004.
9 The view later adopted by Aquinas.
10 E.g. Xenophanes. DK21 Fr. B25 and 26.
11 Plato, *Republic* 380df.
12 Augustine, *City of God* XII.18; *Confessions* XI.10.
13 Augustine, *Confessions* VIII.2.
14 It has been strongly maintained by Pierre Hadot that these ideas go back primarily to Porphyry. He has also linked the *Anonymous Commentary on the Parmenides* with them and claimed Porphyrian authorship for this work. There remains, however, some doubt as to

whether this work is by Porphyry himself and whether its ideas are as clearly demarcated as Hadot interprets them.

15 Augustine, *City of God* VIII.12.
16 *City of God* IX.10.
17 Augustine, *Confessions* VII.20. See also VII.9.
18 E.g. Porphyry, *Sententiae* 35 'That which is greater in bulk is less in power.'
19 Augustine, *On the Magnitude of the Soul* 4.
20 *On the Magnitude of the Soul* 5.
21 *On the Magnitude of the Soul* 28.
22 *Ibid.* 28. Note the combination of Neoplatonic (pouring out the soul into the senses, inner and outer man) and scriptural (child of God, new and old man) themes.
23 *On the Magnitude of the Soul* 36 (80).
24 *Confessions* X.6.
25 Plato, *Theaetetus* 155c–d.
26 Augustine, *Confessions* 8.
27 *Confessions* 8.
28 *Confessions* 16.
29 *Confessions* 16.
30 *Confessions* 27.
31 *Confessions* 17.
32 *Confessions* IX.10.
33 *Confessions* VII.5.7.
34 *Confessions* VII.12.
35 Augustine, *On the Magnitude of the Soul* 24 (45).
36 Augustine, *De Genesi ad litteram* 12.6.(15).
37 Plotinus, *Enneads* IV.6.2. See chapter 4, pp.49f.
38 Augustine, *Confessions* XI.20.
39 *Confessions* XI.26.
40 *sempiterna*, Augustine, *Confessions* IX.10.
41 Augustine, *On the Magnitude of the Soul* 33 (76).
42 He refers in *Orationes* 31.5 to the Platonists 'who have thought best about god and are nearest to us'.
43 Maximus, *de hominis opificio*, *Patrologia Graeca* 44, 205C. Passage as translated by Hilary Armstrong in *St Augustine and Christian Platonism*, (Villanova, PA: Villanova University Press 1967), p.52. Armstrong points out the similarity with the thought of Teilhard de Chardin who also links the salvation and spiritualisation of the universe with the spiritual effort of the individual soul.
44 Synesius, *Hymn* 1.571–574; *On Dreams* 159,14f. (Terzaghi).
45 Gregory of Nyssa, *On Virginity* 11.
46 Dionysius, *Mystical Theology*, II,1f.
47 Boethius, *Consolation* 5.6.
48 He also uses *sempiternus* 'sempiternal'.

49 They are found (in Greek) later in Simplicius, *Commentary on Aristotle's Physics* 1155,13 and in Olympiodorus, *Commentary on Aristotle's Metereologica* 146,15–23.

50 Boethius, *Consolation* 5.6.

SUGGESTIONS FOR FURTHER READING

Many of the texts of the Neoplatonists are not translated into English. I have listed the main texts referred to in this volume, indicating translations where they are available. The most complete collection of the works of the Christian Fathers will be found in *Patrologia Latina* for Latin texts and for the Greek Fathers *Patrologia Graeca* which provides a Greek text and Latin translation. In the list of secondary works I have limited myself to a selection of the most accessible books. The more detailed bibliographies contained in them will provide further material for those who wish to pursue particular topics.

TEXTS

Part I

Plotinus

The standard edition of the Greek text of Plotinus is that of Paul Henry and Edward Schwyzer, *Plotini Opera* in three volumes, Brouwer (Paris and Bruxelles 1951–1973). They also produced a text with some changes and improvements in the Oxford Classical Texts series (*editio minor*) in three volumes, 1964–1982.

The most celebrated English translation is that of Stephen McKenna (1917–1930), which is a work of literature in its own right and, though inaccurate in places, richly communicates the multivalence of Plotinus' prose. The full text is published by Faber and Faber, London 1962. There is an abridged version, edited with introduction and notes by John Dillon, published by Penguin, London 1991. I have sometimes used McKenna's translations in this volume. The Loeb edition in seven volumes, with Greek text and facing English translation by Hilary Armstrong, Heinemann (London 1966–1988), provides the most accessible and clear English translation. It is the translation I have relied on most in this volume, although I have occasionally made minor changes.

Part II

Aeneas of Gaza

Works, *Patrologia Graeca* vol. 85.

Anonymous Commentary on Plato's 'Parmenides'

The Greek text with a French translation may be found in volume 2 of Pierre Hadot's Porphyre et Victorinus, Études Augustiniennes (Paris 1968). There is also an English translation and commentary by Gerald Bechtle, *The Anonymous Commentary on Plato's 'Parmenides'*, Paul Haupt (Bern 1999).

Augustine

Confessions, translated by R. S. Pine-Coffin, Penguin (London 1961).
Confessiones, ed. M. Skutella, Teubner (Leipzig 1981).
City of God, translated by David Knowles, Penguin (London 1972).
De Civitate Dei, eds B. Dombart and A. Kalb, Teubner (Leipzig 1928).
The Magnitude of the Soul, in *The Fathers of the Church* Vol. 4, Catholic University of America Press (Washington DC 1977).
De Quantitate Animae, Latin text and French translation by Pierre de Labriolle, in *Oeuvres de Saint Augustin* Vol. V, de Brouwer (Paris 1948).

Basil

English translation of the *Hexameron* in Vol. VIII of *The Nicene and Post Nicene Fathers*, Eerdmans (Michigan 1975 reprint).
Works, *Patrologia Graeca* 29–32.

Boethius

The Consolation of Philosophy, translated with an introduction and notes by V. E. Watts, Penguin (London 1969).
De Consolatione Philosophiae, ed. W. Weinberger, Corpus Scriptorum Ecclesiasticorum Latinorum 67.

Dionysius (Pseudo-Dionysius)

The Divine Names and The Mystical Theology, translated by C. E. Rolt, SPCK (London 1972).
Works, *Patrologia Graeca* 3.

Gregory of Nazianzen

English translations of select works in Vol. VII of *The Nicene and Post Nicene Fathers*, Eerdmans (Michigan 1972 reprint).
Works, *Patrologia Graeca* 35–38.

Gregory of Nyssa

English translations of select works in Vols. V–VI of *The Nicene and Post Nicene Fathers*, Eerdmans (Michigan 1972– reprints).
Opera Omnia, ed. Jaeger, Brill (Leiden 1960–).
Works, *Patrologia Graeca* 44–46.

Iamblichus

De Anima, text, translation and commentary by John F. Finamore and John M. Dillon, Brill (Leiden 2002).
Iamblichi Chaldcidensis in Platonis Dialogos Commentariorum Fragmenta, edited with translation and commentary by John M. Dillon, Brill (Leiden 1973).
Les Mystères d'Égypte, Greek text, French translation and notes, ed. E. Des Places, Budé (Paris 1966).

Julian

The Works of the Emperor Julian, in 3 vols, Greek text and translation by W. C. Wright, Heinemann (London 1980–1990).

Marinus

Life of Proclus in *Neoplatonic Saints: The Lives of Plotinus and Proclus by their Students*, translated with introduction and notes by Mark Edwards, Liverpool University Press (Liverpool 2000).

Maximus Confessor

Works, *Patrologia Graeca* 90–91.

Philoponus

Against Aristotle on the Eternity of the World, translated by C. Wildberg, Duckworth (London 1987).

De Aeternitate Mundi contra Proclum, ed. H. Rabe, Leipzig 1899.

Porphyry

The most readily available Greek texts are in the Teubner series, but the Budé series provides a Greek text, notes and French translation.

Life of Plotinus in Neoplatonic Saints: The Lives of Plotinus and Proclus by their Students, translated with introduction and notes by Mark Edwards, Liverpool University Press (Liverpool 2000).

Porphyry on Abstinence from Killing Animals, translated with notes by Gillian Clark, Duckworth (London 2000).

Porphyre: de l'Abstinence I, eds. J. Bouffartigue and M. Patillon, Budé (Paris 1977).

Porphyre: de l'Abstinence II–III, eds. J. Bouffartigue and M. Patillon, Budé (Paris 1979).

Porphyrii Opuscula Selecta, ed. A. Nauck, Teubner (Leipzig 1986, reprinted 1963), contains the Greek text of the *Life of Pythagoras, de Abstinentia, ad Marcellam, de Antro Nympharum.*

Porphyrii Sententiae ad Intelligibilia Ducentes, ed. E. Lamberz, Teubner (Leipzig 1975).

Porphyre: Vie de Pythagore, Lettre à Marcella, ed. E. Des Places, Budé (Paris 1982).

Porphyrii Fragmenta, ed. A. Smith, Teubner (Leipzig/Stuttgart 1993).

Proclus

The Elements of Theology, Greek text, translation, introduction and commentary by E. R. Dodds, Oxford 1963 (revised edition). This is still one of the best introductions to Proclus. The commentary provides much comparative material on basic Neoplatonic ideas.

Théologie Platonicienne, eds. H. D. Saffrey and L. G. Westerink, 6 vols., Budé (Paris 1968–1997).

Proclus' Commentary on Plato's Parmenides, translated by Glenn R. Morrow and John M. Dillon, Princeton University Press (Princeton 1987).

Sallustius

Sallustius Concerning the Gods and the Universe, ed. with translation and notes by A. D. Nock, Cambridge 1926 (reprinted Hildesheim 1966).

Synesius

The Letters of Synesius of Cyrene, trans. A. Fitzgerald, Humphrey Milford (London 1926).

Hymnes, ed. Christian Lacombrade, Budé (Paris 1978).

Victorinus

Traités Théologiques sur la Trinité, 2 vols, text and French translation, eds Paul Henry and Pierre Hadot, Édition du Cerf (Paris 1960).

SECONDARY READING

General accounts

Armstrong, A. H., ed., *The Cambridge History of Later Greek and Early Medieval Philosophy*, Cambridge University Press (Cambridge 1967).

Dillon, John M., *The Middle Platonists*, Duckworth (London 1977).

Wallis, R. T., *Neoplatonism*, Duckworth (London, second edn 1995). Contains an updated bibliography by Lloyd P. Gerson.

Wallis, R. T. and Bregman, J. (eds), *Neoplatonism and Gnosticism* (Albany, NY 1992).

Other works

Carabine, Deirdre, *The Unknown God: Negative Theology in the Platonic Tradition: Plato to Eriugena* (Louvain 1995).

Gerson, Lloyd P. (ed.), *The Cambridge Companion to Plotinus*, Cambridge University Press (Cambridge 1996).

Haase, W. and Temporini, H. (eds), *Aufstieg und Niedergang der römischen Welt*, (Berlin/New York 1987), II. 36.1 and 36.2 contain survey, bibliographical and specialist contributions on later Greek philosophy.

O'Meara, John J., *The Young Augustine*, Longman (London 1954).

Sorabji, R., *Time, Creation and the Continuum*, Duckworth (London 1983).

Sorabji, R. (ed.), *Aristotle Transformed: the Ancient Commentators and their Influence*, Duckworth (London 1990).

Zaehner, R.C., *Mysticism Sacred and Profane*, Oxford 1957.

INDEX